BEING
ADOPTED

BEING ADOPTED

The
Lifelong Search for Self

David M. Brodzinsky, Ph.D.
Marshall D. Schechter, M.D.
Robin Marantz Henig

Anchor Books
DOUBLEDAY
NEW YORK   LONDON   TORONTO   SYDNEY   AUCKLAND

AN ANCHOR BOOK

PUBLISHED BY DOUBLEDAY

A DIVISION OF BANTAM DOUBLEDAY DELL PUBLISHING GROUP, INC.
666 FIFTH AVENUE, NEW YORK, NEW YORK 10103

ANCHOR BOOKS, DOUBLEDAY, and the portrayal of an anchor
are trademarks of Doubleday, a division of Bantam Doubleday
Dell Publishing Group, Inc.

Being Adopted was originally published in hardcover by
Doubleday in 1992. The Anchor Books edition is
published by arrangement with Doubleday.

Book design by *Patrice Fodero*

Library of Congress Cataloging-in-Publication Data
Brodzinsky, David.
Being adopted : the lifelong search for self / David M.
Brodzinsky, Marshall D. Schechter, Robin Marantz Henig. — 1st
Anchor Books ed.
p. cm.
Includes bibliographical references and index.
1. Adoptees—Psychology. 2. Children, Adopted—Psychology.
3. Life cycle, Human. 4. Maturation (Psychology). 5. Socialization.
I. Schechter, Marshall D. II. Henig, Robin Marantz. III. Title.
[HV875.B74 1993]
155.2—dc20 92-38103
CIP

ISBN 0-385-41426-9
Copyright © *1992 by David M. Brodzinsky, Marshall D. Schechter,*
and Robin Marantz Henig
ALL RIGHTS RESERVED
PRINTED IN THE UNITED STATES OF AMERICA
FIRST ANCHOR BOOKS EDITION: April 1993

1 3 5 7 9 10 8 6 4 2

To Anne, where it all began

——DMB

With love to my wife, Ann,
whose experiences with adoption have helped
shape my own

——MDS

To Norman Brenner, my uncle, in loving
memory

——RMH

CONTENTS

"I'm a Dopted"—Parroting the Adoption Story
The Adoptive Bond
Special Cases: Later Adoptions
Emergence of Racial Awareness

3. *Middle Childhood—Ages Six to Twelve*   61

A Sense of the Self
Self-Esteem and the Sense of Mastery
The Growth of Logical Thought
Grieving for the Lost Family
The Family Romance Fantasy
The "Search" Begins—In the Imagination
The Pain of Being Different
The Resilient Child
A Special Case: Learning Disabilities
More Special Cases: Late-Placed or International
    Adoptees

4. *Adolescence—Ages Thirteen to Nineteen*   93

Are Teenagers in Turmoil?
Universal Changes of Adolescence
How Do I Look?
Resolving the Identity Crisis
The Family Romance Fantasy Continues
Sexual Expression and the "Bad Seed"
First Signs of an Active Search for Birth Parents
Moving Toward Adulthood

PART II. THE ADOPTED ADULT

5. *Young Adulthood—The Twenties and Thirties*   123

When Are You a "Grown-Up"?
A Dialectical Thinking Style
The Search for Identity Continues
Seeking and Achieving Intimacy
Parenthood: Undoing Past Mistakes
Pursuing a Career Identity
The Search: Who, When, and Why

PROLOGUE

Being adopted means different things to different people. To Ruth, fifty-five, it is the sense of always feeling unsettled, of there being an unfinished chapter to her life. To Stuart, twenty-seven, it is gratitude at having been raised by loving and generous parents instead of by a birth mother he knows could never have given him what he needed. And to Kelli, twenty-six, it is the continuous pain of feeling different, out of place, never fully human.

There is, in short, no "right" or "wrong" way to experience being adopted. But if you are adopted, you will think about that fact of your life now and again—maybe when a question arises about your genetic background, maybe when you encounter a particularly rough spot in your life, maybe every single day.

We wrote this book with one primary goal in mind: to map out what it is like to be adopted. *Being Adopted* is different from most other adoption books you might have seen. It is not a how-to book, nor is it a parenting book. It is not a book about searching for birth parents, or talking to children about being adopted, or changing society's attitudes toward adoption. It is not a polemic calling for the opening up of the adoption process or the unsealing of birth records—although these are, for reasons we will outline, goals that we embrace.

Instead, this book is a way to share our model of normal adjustment to being adopted as it occurs throughout the life span. As we take you, step-by-step, through the life span, we will examine the ups and downs of psychological adaptation that can be predicted for even the most well-adjusted of adoptees.

We base our model on our professional experiences, accumulated over a combined total of fifty-five years of clinical and research work with adoptees and their families. To amplify these clinical impressions

1

and research conclusions, we include the stories of adoptees who have successfully—and occasionally not so successfully—incorporated the fact of being adopted into their own lifelong search for self.

OUR SIX THEMES

Six themes run throughout the book. The first relates to narrative structure: our focus will be on the experience of adoption *through the eyes of adoptees*. We intend to describe the conscious and unconscious thoughts, beliefs, feelings, fantasies, and desires of those who know adoption best—the people who live it day in and day out, from the time they first are able to reflect on their unique family status until old age, when there is a final effort to integrate adoption into a more complete sense of self. By contrast, the experiences of adoptive parents and birth parents—the two other points of the "adoption triangle"—will receive little attention in our book. This is not because their perspectives are unimportant, but only because we must maintain a manageable focus.

The second theme revolves around the *developmental perspective*. The experience of adoption—like any other experience—is not static. It changes with time as the forces of development shape and reshape the way we think, feel, relate, and grow. Thus, the meaning and implications of being adopted, to the individual, are bounded by time and circumstances. How it feels to be adopted at the age of four is different from how it feels at the age of eight, sixteen, twenty-five, forty, or seventy-five. In our book, we illustrate the common developmental pathways on the road to adoption adjustment.

Our third theme is *normality*. The developmental experiences we describe are essentially normal. An individual may experience them in exactly the same way as the people in this book—or she may not. Wide ranges of ups and downs fall within the scheme of what we consider to be a perfectly healthy adjustment to the fact of being adopted. But even though these ups and downs are normal, some of our stories will represent extremes. To highlight the variations in adjustment to adoption that occur over the life cycle, we have deliberately chosen some stories from people who, for a while, were *not* making a healthy adjustment—either to adoption or to other issues in their lives. These are our patients, who sought us out because their attempts at resolution were, for one reason or another, just not working. They are the extremes of what normal adoptees go through too.

The notion of variability brings us to our fourth theme: *individuality*. Just as it is important to appreciate the common, if not universal, patterns of adjustment that emerge for adoptees, it is also necessary to recognize that no two humans are alike—whether adopted or not. Moreover, the experience of adoption will be shaped by the way the issue is discussed, or not discussed, in the adoptive home. The important point is this: there is no single "right way" to experience adoption.

The *search for self* is the fifth theme of the book. Although the definition of self is a much-debated concept, it is at the heart of all personality theories. The struggle to understand who you are, where you fit in, and how you feel about yourself is universal. It is a unique part of being human. Self-reflection is one process that sets us apart from other animals. The search for self is not restricted to adolescents going through the much-touted "identity crisis"; it begins at birth and continues through old age, with many ups and downs along the way to resolution. Indeed, just when the issue seems resolved, something usually happens to churn everything up again. Adoptees go through the search for self in some unique and characteristic ways, and many of the differences can be explained by the fact that adoption cuts off people from a part of themselves.

When we are cut off from something important to us, we experience *a sense of loss*—the sixth major theme of this book. Loss is an inherent part of life—a "necessary" part, as writer Judith Viorst has put it.[1] From the moment we lose the comfort and security of the womb until the day we lose our lives, we encounter innumerable events associated with loss. They range from the minor—getting turned down for a part in the school play—to the major—the death of a spouse or parent. Every loss shapes us. We are shaped too by the process of grieving that commonly follows loss. Adoptees are no different from others in this regard. And yet, as we will see, the resolution of loss, and the ability to grieve successfully, are often complicated for adoptees. To understand the psychology of adoption from the perspective of the adoptee is to recognize and appreciate the unique role played by loss and grieving in the search for self.

As you read this book, remember that one's inner life is constantly in flux—including "adjustment" to the fact of being adopted. Just as people don't mature once and then stay the same for the rest of their lives, they also don't wake up one day finished with thinking about adoption. The path to psychological maturity may look, at first glance, as though it's straight and narrow. But it usually turns out to be littered with rocky spots and obstacles that you must work your way through, or around, before setting off again on a path that once again seems smooth. Whenever the road ahead looks smooth, though, you're sure to find that smoothness only exists until the next rocky spot.

That's what happens too in dealing with adoption: it's an issue that emerges, seems to be settled, and then reemerges at some later point along life's path.

THE VOICES OF ADOPTEES

"I didn't like being chosen," writes Susanna, forty-four. "And I didn't like having to be so good all the time for fear they [my adoptive parents] would get rid of me too. I didn't like being different from regular people."

Quotes like Susanna's come from our research with nonclinical populations, as well as from the clinical work we do with our patients. They also come from questionnaires sent out to adult adoptees specifically for the purpose of this book. Although some of these adoptees are members of "search" organizations or other advocacy groups, most are just ordinary folks who answered our newspaper advertisements seeking volunteers willing to share their thoughts about being adopted. Approximately one hundred people responded to our request for volunteers.[2]

In soliciting these individuals, our goal was to augment the insights and conclusions derived from the adult adoptee research literature—which focuses mostly on support-group members or psychotherapy patients—as well as from the clinical literature and our own clinical impressions. We wanted to provide a more balanced view of what it is like for adults who have grown up being adopted. Yet we don't want to fool ourselves or our readers into believing that these individuals represent a cross-section of all adults who are adopted. People volunteer for research and fill out questionnaires for all sorts of reasons. The people we heard from are more likely to define themselves in terms of their adoption than are people we never heard from.

In examining the autobiographical sketches we received, though, we are convinced that while our sample is not random or totally representative, it is certainly useful. Struck by the diversity of their stories, and by certain common themes that connected them, we try to give the reader a flavor of both in the case histories that follow.

The quotes we use are real, but the names, circumstances, and settings have been changed to preserve confidentiality—with the exception of a few prominent adoption advocates who wanted their points of view expressed.

A PERSONAL NOTE

Although none of the authors is adopted, we all know adoptees well, as members of our own families, as friends and neighbors, as research subjects, as patients. Among the three of us we have one spouse, one stepchild, and two first cousins who are adopted. And in the course of our research and clinical work, we have interviewed or treated thousands of adoptees, ranging in age from infancy through the eighties. All these personal experiences have gone into the writing of *Being Adopted*.

Professionally, we come to this book from three different perspectives. Marshall, a child psychiatrist, is professor emeritus at the University of Pennsylvania. Much of his professional research and writing, as well as his clinical practice, has focused on adoption-related issues. David, a clinical developmental psychologist, is associate professor of psychology at Rutgers University, where for the past thirteen years he has been studying the adjustment of adopted children and their families. Like Marshall, much of his clinical practice is with members of the adoption triangle. David and Marshall are coeditors of a professional textbook called *The Psychology of Adoption*, published in 1990 by Oxford University Press. Robin, a journalist, is the author of three previous books and dozens of magazine and newspaper articles on topics ranging from adoption to liposuction, from fetal surgery to senility.

Our different perspectives allow us to combine a clinical feel for the deviant, a research orientation toward both normal and abnormal processes, and a journalistic appreciation of the life stories of individuals.

To avoid the clunky "he/she" nonsexist pronoun common in many enlightened books these days, we have chosen another route that we hope achieves the same ends without sacrificing literary style. When referring to a gender-neutral adoptee, we alternate the use of "he" and "she" from one chapter to the next. We find this compromise less jarring than some of the alternatives with which we experimented. For the same reason, we have chosen on occasion to use the term "adoptee" because of its brevity. We apologize to those readers who might feel that the term depersonalizes the adopted individual.

INTRODUCTION: THE CONTEXT OF ADOPTION

As recently as a generation ago, being adopted seemed no different from being born into the family that raised you. We used to think that parents simply chose and received a perfect baby, told her at the age of three or four that she was adopted, and then went on to live a family life that looked just like Ozzie and Harriet's. Being told about adoption, went the thinking of the 1950s, was like being told about sex: the subject was raised, carefully and appropriately, at the right stage in the child's development, and then it never needed to be raised again.

Now we know better—not only about sex, but about adoption too. Now we know that being adopted can be something that colors a person's relationship with her adoptive parents, her emerging sense of self, and the intimate relationships she forges for the rest of her life. Now we know that the issue of being adopted is one that will be returned to, consciously and unconsciously, at various points in an adoptee's growth and development.

And now we know how important it is to consider not just the internal life of the adoptee, but the social context in which she is raised.

ADOPTION: SOLUTION OR RISK?

When looked at in the greater scheme of things, adoption is a wonderful solution. It solves the problem of the adoptive parents, people who—because of infertility or other complications—cannot have the families they had dreamed of. It solves the problem of the birth parents, who are facing an unplanned, unwanted pregnancy. And it solves the problem of the adoptee, who otherwise would be without a home and a sense of permanency.

Many people on the national political scene promote adoption as an alternative to abortion, calling it the best solution to an unplanned pregnancy. A third option, keeping the baby, is barely discussed in these political debates. While we don't aim to address the adoption-not-abortion issue in this book, we can say that based on recent psychological research, adoption is probably a better solution to an unplanned pregnancy—from the point of view of the child's eventual adjustment—than is keeping the child in a birth family that doesn't want her.

International research has compared the development of children reared in a variety of settings: adoptive families, institutions, foster homes, or in birth families in which the mothers had previously applied for abortions and been turned down, or had originally planned to give up their babies for adoption but changed their minds.

In one such study, Michael Bohman, a psychiatrist at the University of Umea in Sweden, and his colleagues studied the development of Swedish children raised in what Bohman called "ambivalent" homes —children whose mothers had registered them for adoption at birth but had subsequently changed their minds.[1] Bohman compared these children with children who were adopted at birth, children raised in permanent foster homes, and children living in the community with their nonambivalent biological parents.

At the age of eleven, the nonadopted children in biological homes showed the lowest rate of emotional and behavioral disturbances, followed by the adopted children. But the most disturbed were the children raised in foster care *and*, significantly, the children raised by biological parents who had originally considered putting them up for adoption. This finding goes against the conventional wisdom that the biological family, no matter how unwilling it is to keep a child, is always better than any alternative.

A similar conclusion was reached by Henry P. David, a psychologist at the University of Maryland, who looked at the legacy of being "born unwanted" in a slightly different way.[2] David studied children in Czechoslovakia born to mothers who had twice been denied abortions by governmental authorities. Children raised by these "resistant mothers," he found, were at increased risk for emotional and behavioral difficulties, minimal brain dysfunction, and academic under-achievement. Even in young adulthood, they suffered reduced life satisfaction, less job satisfaction, difficulty in love relationships, increased criminality, and other problems.

But even though being adopted is better for a child than is being raised in an ambivalent home, foster care, or an institution, it is not perfect; it carries complications and difficulties of its own. Because of the long tradition of viewing adoption as a solution to many problems, professionals and lay people have had trouble accepting the possibility that the solution itself could at times be a problem. But we believe that knowing about the complications that can be expected will help adoptees, their parents, and the professional community better deal with them as they arise.

The vast majority of adoptees do perfectly well in all of the ways that society measures success. They grow up, they marry, they have families of their own. They relate well to their friends and their adoptive families. They hold down jobs, have hobbies, have long sweet moments of love and happiness. Indeed, research indicates that about 85 percent of adoption placements are viewed, in retrospect, as "successful" by family members and the professionals who counsel them.[3]

But problems do emerge in an adoptee's life, usually in a predictable and understandable way. We and many other clinicians and researchers have found a pattern in normal adoption adjustment: when adoption arises as a salient issue in a person's inner life, the most pervasive feeling is an overwhelming sense of loss. The loss inherent in adoption is unlike other losses we have come to expect in a lifetime, such as death or divorce. Adoption loss is more pervasive, less socially recognized, and more profound.[4]

Usually, no differences in adoptees' patterns of adjustment are seen in infancy and the preschool years. When problems do arise, they tend to occur in the elementary school years and in adolescence. Research studies have not found any increased problems in children younger than about five or six (if they were adopted as infants),[5] and the evidence is unclear about whether adopted adults (again, those adopted as infants) are more at risk for problems than nonadopted adults.

For children between six and eighteen, though, a number of studies have shown that being adopted is a risk factor for having certain psychological problems, especially low self-esteem, academic problems, and a range of rebellious activities known as "acting out" behaviors: aggression, stealing, lying, hyperactivity, oppositional behavior, and running away.[6] The clustering of certain symptoms in troubled adoptees actually led some researchers, in the early 1980s, to theorize the existence of an "adopted child syndrome." [7] Few professionals today believe such a syndrome exists.

What has been observed, however, is that adopted children and adolescents make up a higher-than-expected proportion of children in psychological distress. Only 1 to 2 percent of the population under age eighteen are adopted by non–blood relatives, yet adoptees comprise an unusually high proportion of children involved in outpatient psychotherapy (5 percent rather than the expected 1 or 2 percent), young patients in residential treatment centers and psychiatric hospitals (10 to 15 percent instead of 1 or 2 percent), and children identified by school systems as either perceptually, neurologically, or emotionally impaired (6 to 9 percent instead of 1 or 2 percent).[8]

One recent study by Nicholas Zill, a researcher at the Washington organization Child Trend, found that adopted children were three times as likely as nonadoptees of the same age to have been treated by a psychologist or psychiatrist in the previous year.[9]

Of course, there are many ways to account for statistics like these. Adoptive parents usually are middle-class or upper-middle-class, and accustomed to making use of people in the "helping professions," many of whom they encountered on the road to adopting a child in the first place. So they may be especially quick to seek professional help at the first sign of trouble.

And while the bulk of the research indicates that adoptees are more vulnerable to psychological problems, not every study has come up with these findings. Bohman's Swedish study of "ambivalent" mothers, for example, noted more problems among adoptees than nonadoptees at the age of eleven, but the differences disappeared by the age of fifteen, and no differences were seen at ages eighteen or twenty-three.[10] Before we can make any categorical statements about adoption adjustment, we will have to figure out why a significant minority of researchers have reached such different conclusions.

In looking at all the data, including the contradictory data, we believe there is indeed a clear tendency among adoptees not only to *seek* professional help, but also to *need* it. And we believe the increased vulnerability of adoptees to psychological problems can be explained largely by their experience of loss.

The Losses of Adoption

Sarah was a perfectly happy, well-adjusted seventeen-year-old who had been adopted as an infant. She always knew she was adopted, and always felt comfortable and loved in her adoptive family. Nonetheless, Sarah had a vague sense of longing, a feeling similar to sensations we've heard described by hundreds of other adopted acquaintances and patients.

> "Sometimes I feel incomplete," Sarah told us. "I need to know more: Why did it happen? What is she like? Who is my birth father? What is he like? The older I get, the more important it is to know. It's pretty frustrating being an adoptee sometimes."

There's nothing abnormal or unexpected about Sarah's frustration. The process that accounts for her feelings, in large part, is grief for the parents she so often wonders about. Such grieving is, essentially, what we see happening in most adoptees who, like Sarah, are weathering one of those rocky spots in psychological development. Indeed, we believe that much of what has been called pathological in an adoptee's behavior is little more than the unrecognized manifestation of an adaptive grieving process.

This perspective has been readily accepted as an explanation for why children adopted *after* the first year or so of life often run into problems later. When a child forms attachments to her first caretakers, whether biological parents, relatives, or foster parents, and then is removed from their care and placed in a new home, it is almost inevitable that she will experience a sense of loss and will grieve for them.

Grieving almost always follows loss. It has many emotional and behavioral manifestations: shock, anger, depression, despair, helplessness, hopelessness. Grief can be blocked or it can be prolonged, but usually it is a normal and adaptive response to the experience of loss.

For children adopted late, the loss can be traumatic and overt, placing great stress on the child. But for children adopted at birth, there is still loss involved. It is less traumatic, less overt, but it can shape the child's entire personality. Adoptees who are placed in the first days or weeks of life grieve not only for the parents they never knew, but for the other aspects of themselves that have been lost through adoption: the loss of origins, of a completed sense of self, of genealogical continuity. Adoptees might feel a loss too of their sense of stability in their relationship with their *adoptive* parents; if one set of parents can relinquish them, they might think, then why can't another?

The loss for early-placed adoptees, though, is generally not acute or traumatic, nor is it usually consciously experienced until the age of five or so. It emerges gradually, as the child's cognitive understanding of adoption begins to unfold. And it can lead to subtle behavioral changes in childhood that seem at first glance to have nothing whatever to do with loss and grieving.

Sometimes grieving becomes a significant factor in an adoptee's life; sometimes it doesn't. Some adoptees are overwhelmed with feelings of alienation and disconnection. Others, for reasons we still don't fully understand, have no such feelings, and are instead intensely grateful for having been given the safe and loving homes their adoptive parents made for them.

We can't predict which adoptee will feel incomplete or abandoned and which will feel cherished, which will choose to emphasize the "lost" nature of adoption and which will dwell only on the "found." But we *can* say that both types of reactions are understandable, common, and usually part of a healthy adaptation—and that they can exist, at different points along the life span, in the same individual.

THE LIFELONG SEARCH FOR SELF

For the adoptee, the experience of loss is usually felt in the context of the search for self. The concept of the self is central to the notion of personality; on this point most personality theorists would agree. But it would be hard to get them to agree on exactly what "the self" is. When we use the term, we mean the way in which an individual views herself—something that's often called "self-concept."

Typically, a sense of self is thought to require an element of self-reflection, a consciousness that can't exist without words or symbols. A self-concept, the thinking goes, comes when a person can almost step out of her body and look at herself to form an image. But as we will see in the next chapter, there are some aspects of the self that begin in infancy, long before a child is capable of this symbolic self-reflection.

Different theorists have conceptualized the self in various ways. Our own notions of the self include several components. There is the *physical self*, which includes awareness and perceptions of one's own body: how it looks, how it feels, how it sounds, smells, tastes. There is the *psychological self*, which includes our notions of our own intangible qualities, including what we call our personalities: our view of our intelligence, our capacity for empathy, our ability to control impulses, our generosity or lack of generosity.

There is the *social self*, which includes our awareness of ourselves in relation to others and our view of how others see us. This includes whether we feel liked, whether we think we are considered attractive, whether we believe others think us to be kind or friendly or empathetic.

And there is the overriding, evaluative component of the self that integrates the other three: the part called *self-esteem*. This represents our judgments about whether aspects of our selves are good or bad, likable or dislikable, valuable or not. Self-esteem plays a major role in patterns of psychological adjustment. To feel good about yourself fosters healthy development; to feel bad about yourself—especially about a component of yourself that you value—tends to undermine psychological well-being.

The search for self is universal and ongoing. For adoptees and nonadoptees alike, an understanding of the self is one of the primary tasks of psychological development. Our sense of who we are is influenced by every experience we have; it's changed each time our life circumstances change. And it's not just major life events—birth, death, marriage, adoption—that have an effect on our sense of self. The accumulation of small events that we often take for granted—every compliment, every rejection, every accomplishment, every failure—contributes to our self-perception.

As many authorities in the adoption field have noted, adoptees have a particularly complex task in their search for self.[11] When you live with your biological family, you have guideposts to help you along. You can see bits of your own future reflected in your parents, pieces of your own personality echoed in your brothers and sisters.

There are fewer such clues for someone who is adopted. Adoptees often talk about certain "cutoffs" in their history—from their birth parents, their extended birth family, their awareness of their genetic inheritance, and sometimes their ethnic or racial origins. The British researcher H. J. Sants coined the term "genealogical bewilderment" in 1964 to describe this sense of disconnectedness from the past.[12] For most adoptees, bewilderment is not a chronic condition. It is a sense of confusion and alienation that seems to emerge at critical times in a person's development.

Birthdays are often one such critical time. The day Nate turned ten, he wondered about his biological mother, "Does she think of me on my birthday?" For Carl, age fifteen, birthdays had always been a source of confusion, awkwardness, and embarrassment. "It's pretty weird for me then, being the center of attention," he says. "I feel like a fake. Everyone is around and celebrating the day I was born, making a big deal about it, and they weren't even there for it." And as Francie's twenty-third birthday approached—her birth mother's age when Francie was born—she asked herself, "Was she happy, or did she have an empty feeling as I do?"

But the confusion can last for much longer than a birthday; it can last through long periods of an adoptee's life. Indeed, because questions about the past loom so large, some adoptees have trouble forging ahead into the future, and instead get stuck on a particular developmental stage. Even at the age of thirty-five, for example, our patient Jocelyn told us, "Not knowing where I came from seems to hold me back from developing myself."

ADOPTION ADJUSTMENT ACROSS THE LIFE SPAN

In the chapters that follow, we will look at the ways in which these two crucial processes—the search for self and the experience of loss—show themselves at different periods in the adoptee's psychological development. Our primary emphasis will be on the "traditional adoption" in which an infant younger than six months of age is placed with a nonrelated family. Along the way, though, we will also examine the experience of adoption from the perspective of children who are adopted at older ages, from foreign countries, or with certain handicaps that make them qualify as "special needs" adoptees.

There are many ways of conceptualizing adoption adjustment. We've chosen to do so by utilizing Erik Erikson's model of the life cycle. Erikson, a Danish-born psychoanalyst, developed a seven-stage model describing the salient psychosocial tasks that confront people as they move from infancy through old age.[13] His assumption is that these tasks are universal. Our assumption is that they apply for adoptees and nonadoptees alike—but with some important differences.

As Table 1 shows, Erikson envisioned each stage in life as the conflict of two competing directions. When the conflict is resolved and the individual moves on to the next developmental stage, the issues recede in importance. But they never disappear. We are forever struggling with the issues we seem to have resolved at an earlier period of life.

Table 1   A Psychosocial Model of Adoption Adjustment[14]

Age Period	Erikson's Psychosocial Tasks	Adoption-Related Tasks
Infancy[a]	Trust vs. Mistrust	Adjusting to transition to a new home
		Developing secure attachments, especially in cases of delayed placement
Toddlerhood and Preschool Years[b]	Autonomy vs. Shame and Doubt; Initiative vs. Guilt	Learning about birth and reproduction
		Adjusting to initial information about adoption
		Recognizing differences in physical appearance, especially in interracial and intercountry adoption
Middle Childhood	Industry vs. Inferiority	Understanding the meaning and implications of being adopted
		Searching for answers regarding one's origin and the reasons for relinquishment
		Coping with physical differences from family members
		Coping with stigma associated with adoption

Age Period	Erikson's Psycho-social Tasks	Adoption-Related Tasks
		Coping with peer reactions to adoption
		Coping with adoption-related loss
Adolescence	Ego Identity vs. Identity Confusion	Further exploration of the meaning and implications of being adopted
		Connecting adoption to one's sense of identity
		Coping with racial identity in cases of interracial adoption
		Coping with physical differences from family members
		Resolving the family romance fantasy
		Coping with adoption-related loss, especially as it relates to the sense of self
		Considering the possibility of searching for biological family
Young Adulthood	Intimacy vs. Isolation	Further exploration of the implications of adoption as it relates to the growth of self and the development of intimacy
		Further considerations of searching; beginning the search
		Adjusting to parenthood in light of the history of one's relinquishment
		Facing one's unknown genetic history in the context of the birth of children
		Coping with adoption-related loss

Age Period	Erikson's Psycho-social Tasks	Adoption-Related Tasks
Middle Adult-hood	Generativity vs. Stagnation	Further exploration of the implications of adoption as it relates to the aging self
		Reconciling the creation of a psychological legacy with one's unknown past
		Further considerations of searching
		Coping with adoption-related loss
Late Adulthood	Ego Integrity vs. Despair	Final resolution of the implications of adoption in the context of a life review
		Final considerations regarding searching for surviving biological family

[a] There is no conscious awareness of being adopted at this stage.
[b] There is an awareness of being adopted at this stage, but little under-standing of its meaning and implications.

Erikson's life-cycle model provides a framework for the rest of the book. In the next chapter we'll describe infancy, where the primary psychosocial "crisis," in Erikson's view, is Trust versus Mistrust. Chapter Two covers toddlerhood and the preschool years, where the crises are Autonomy versus Shame and Doubt, and Initiative versus Guilt. These two chapters explain the context in which adoption is first introduced to the child, long before she can fully understand it. Although "being adopted" has little meaning to infants and young children, we begin our exploration at this stage because it creates the context in which adoption comes into play at later points in the life span. This helps set the stage for the kind of support the child will receive later, when she starts to struggle with the adoption issue.

Adopted preschoolers tend to have very positive feelings about being adopted. The "adoption story" they are told generally emphasizes the happiness they brought into their parents' lives, and it's told in the context of a warm, loving, and protective family environment.

But as a young child's cognitive powers grow, so does her ability to understand the meaning of being adopted. She can see it as an alternative way of coming into a family, and as she comes to recognize the blood tie between herself and family members who do not live with her, she can understand that she has an entire birth family that is actually related to her.

In Chapter Three, on "middle childhood," we describe the way this realization slowly dawns. The Eriksonian struggle in this period is one between Industry and Inferiority. It is a time of mastery and of understanding the world. Here we'll describe the development of the child's understanding of adoption and its impact on the sense of self and patterns of adjustment. It is at this period of life that the full impact of loss usually is first felt. Now the child can infer the flip side of her beloved "adoption story"—that for her to have been chosen, she first had to have been given away.

For children of this age, adoption implies not just family building, but also family loss. The conscious and unconscious grieving that goes along with that sense of loss accounts for many of the behavioral changes that we and other professionals have noted in elementary-school-age adoptees: increased anger, aggression, oppositional behavior, uncommunicativeness, depression, and self-image problems.

The moment of epiphany regarding the losses of adoption comes for different children at different ages, though it rarely comes before the age of five. The sense of loss that develops now has as its behavioral manifestation the act of grieving. Grieving reemerges at other crucial points along the life span, usually at moments of crisis or change: marriage, the birth of a child, the death of the adoptive parents. We will explore, through case histories, the ways in which renewed grieving can complicate the developmental tasks at each stage.

Chapter Four, on adolescence, explains the Erikson stage of Ego Identity versus Identity Confusion—the famous "identity crisis." During this period, the search for self is especially complicated for adoptees. The primary task of adolescence is separation from the family of origin, as young people develop the resources to venture out alone into the adult world. But adopted teenagers who pull away from their adoptive families always have a phantom biological family from which they must pull away as well. This task is much more difficult; how can you disentangle yourself from something that to you doesn't really exist, or about which you know little or nothing?

In Chapter Five, we focus on the young adult's crisis of Intimacy versus Isolation. Here, too, there are special hurdles for the adoptee to manage. Mark, for instance, never consciously grieved for the loss of his biological parents until he was twenty-eight and his first child was born. "I saw her come out, and the first thing I noticed was her big nose—a nose that looked just like mine," he said. "Then it hit me like a sledgehammer. My daughter was the first blood relative I had ever met."

Chapter Six, on middle adulthood, describes the conflict between Generativity and Stagnation. During this period of life, according to Erikson, the major focus is on leaving behind for the next generation something of yourself. This is characterized by the desire to construct a psychological legacy, either in the form of a literal descendant or through acts of teaching, mentoring, or creating. Often this act of looking forward into the future requires the adoptee to search out details of her own past. "It's one thing to be uncertain about my own history," one middle-aged adoptee told us. "It's quite another thing to be without a history to pass on to my children." This stage of life often means facing again the reality of those "blank spaces" of the adoptee's personal history—of her unknown origin and the myriad unanswered questions that go with it. With an appreciation of the limited time left to live, she may find herself pressing once again for answers.

In Chapter Seven, on late adulthood, we discuss the last psycho-social crisis described by Erikson, Ego Integrity versus Despair. The focus here is on the person's final effort to come to terms with her life. By reviewing the successes and the failures of her life, its pleasures and disappointments, the older adult seeks to achieve a more integrated and meaningful sense of herself. For adoptees, the life review offers one last chance to answer the question of what it has meant to have been adopted. As we shall see, for some individuals the question has remained a focal point of their existence; for others, it is but a vague, ephemeral entity that barely seems connected to them.

Research and clinical experience—our own and others'—suggest that while adoptees must move through these developmental tasks, doing so can be harder for them than for nonadoptees. In the chapters to come, through case histories and research findings, we will describe how and why this is so.

THE IMPACT OF OPEN ADOPTION AND OTHER VARIATIONS

In adoption in the 1990s, anything goes. Childless couples place classified ads in newspapers and interview pregnant women. Birth mothers strike deals where they remain in contact with their babies, in a sort of favorite-aunt capacity. Couples go abroad to adopt babies, or stay at home and adopt babies of different races—thus raising children who look so different from their adoptive parents that strangers will know the family's situation in an instant. Older children or children with "special needs" are adopted by single men or single women desperate for a child.

In some situations, infants from destitute countries are abandoned at the door of the convent, and the circumstances of their life before adoption are unimaginable. In others, letters and videos are exchanged between birth parents and adoptive parents, and everything about the circumstances of the adoption is "open"—so open, in fact, that adoptive parents occasionally even serve as birthing coaches for the mother during the baby's delivery.

The diversity in adoption today has brought about considerable controversy. Much debate has arisen regarding the pros and cons of the various types of adoption. Perhaps the most controversial practice is so-called "open adoption," a term that has come to mean many things to many people. When we use the term here, we mean an ongoing communication among the three points of the "adoption triangle": the birth mother, the adoptive parents, and the adoptee. They may choose different options regarding how extensive they want their contact to be, but the defining feature is that these options are under their control, and ideally are based on full and complete knowledge.

Open adoption is relatively new. The oldest children adopted under open arrangements are just entering their teens, and most are still not out of elementary school.[15] Undoubtedly, the experience of openness will alter the experience of being adopted. If the birth mother is given a name, a face, and a status as a very special member of the extended family, the loss felt by adoptees will not be the same. How it will be felt, though, is still unknown.

Open adoption may turn out to be a great alternative that avoids many of the complications we describe in the chapters to come. Certainly, this is the position of those professionals and parents who advocate greater openness. But it also may create new problems of its own. Opponents of open adoption say the child may fear that her birth mother, who may be a frequent visitor, will change her mind and take her back, or that there will be a hesitancy on the part of both child and adoptive parents to form a true bond with the birth mother looking over their shoulders. Some even say the child may experience a more profound confusion about why she was relinquished if the birth mother keeps showing up.

What we, and others, currently know about being adopted tends to be based on people who were adopted in rather traditional arrangements—adoptions of young infants, by parents of the same race, arranged either independently or through adoption agencies, in which both sets of parents were strangers to each other and remain strangers after the placement. In traditional adoption, the adoption records are "sealed" by the courts and remain confidential. But things are changing in adoption, not only in terms of who is adopting and who is being adopted, but also in terms of the relationship among the three parties involved. So while what we know and describe here is still relevant for adoptees in later childhood, adolescence, and adulthood, it might not really hold for adoptees in the next generation.

We will try, in this book, to take into account the broad range of adoption as it now exists. As adoption becomes more varied—which seems inevitable—it will no doubt become progressively harder to make generalizations about what it's like to be adopted.

In the course of growing up, each of us encounters experiences that will shape us. These become part of our own inner landscapes, issues that are confronted and dealt with and then put away for a while. In many respects, being adopted is no different from any of these other issues.

People can't escape the fact of being adopted any more than they can avoid the fact of being blond or introverted or raised by a single mother. It is part of their personal history; it helped make them who they are.

Sometimes an adoptee will consider it a big deal that she is adopted. At other times, it will seem less significant. But as with any one of the myriad other issues we all face day to day, what it means to her will change. Being an adult includes being able to deal with this psychological ebb and flow. Sometimes we may spend a good deal of our psychic energy working on our marriage relationships, sometimes we fret about our children, sometimes we dwell on our own or our loved ones' physical illnesses or careers or love affairs. We are constantly having to cope with personal issues, both large and small, that is what it means to be a human being.

In explaining this to adoptive parents, who are especially sensitive about the question of what role adoption will play in their children's inner lives, we like to use the metaphor of the hatbox in the closet.

Each of us has things to which we return now and then to work on and worry over—things from the past and present that occasionally resurface and require our attention. It may be a relationship to a sister, it may be a fear of flying, it may be a tragic first love affair or insecurity about our intellectual competence. We tuck these issues away in a hatbox, in a closet, in a far-off corner of the house.

Every now and then, something makes us search out that far-off corner, open the closet door, take down the box, and deal with the issue for a while. Eventually, we feel finished with it, at least for the time being, so we put away the box and go back to living our lives. Some day in the future, though, we'll go back to that closet again, and deal with the issue in the box for a while longer.

That's what the adoption issue is like for most adoptees—no more, no less.

Part I

THE ADOPTED
CHILD

Chapter 1

INFANCY

THE FIRST YEAR OF LIFE

Jon and Nancy were required to wait months before they could bring home their adopted son, Sam, even though they knew who he was and where he was. The policy of the adoption agency was simply that all infants should spend their first three months in foster care. But at least the caseworker told them that everything about Sam was perfectly normal: his mother's pregnancy was normal, his birth was normal, and his time in the foster home was happy and uneventful.

Within a week of coming home, however, Sam seemed far from normal. "I'm not sure how babies are supposed to behave, but I don't think it should be like this," Nancy told her pediatrician in a near-panic. Sam was colicky, had frequent diarrhea, and seemed to cry all the time. Again Nancy changed his formula.

Within another week, Sam had developed a raw rash all over his trunk that sent Nancy rushing to a dermatologist. The specialist could see nothing wrong, though he was concerned enough to order a series of laboratory studies. Everything came back negative. Again Nancy changed his formula.

For three months, Sam was cranky, unhappy, slow to grow, impossible to comfort. Formula changes seemed to make no difference; schedule changes seemed to make no difference; more cuddling or less cuddling seemed to make no difference.

And then suddenly the cloud lifted. At the age of six months, Sam came into his own. He started to smile, was responsive to both Nancy and Jon, gained weight, and—miracle of miracles—slept through the night.

"After it passed, people told us he was just taking his own sweet time getting used to us," Jon said later at an adoptive parents' support-group meeting. "Everything about our home was different from the way his foster home had been, and he was unhappy about that."

Of course, not only did Sam have to adjust to Jon and Nancy, but Jon and Nancy had to adjust to Sam.

We begin our exploration of how it feels to be adopted by describing someone who hasn't a clue that he even *is* adopted—the infant. Only by understanding the context in which the child is being raised from the start can we understand how he will experience the fact of being adopted.

The context of adoption includes a child's socialization environment: the family's structure and general child-rearing practices, the family's adoption-related attitudes and behavior, and the general attitudes about adoption in the larger community. As the sociologist H. David Kirk has suggested, this context can help predict how an individual deals with being adopted.[1] Adoptees handle adoption best, he says, when they are raised by families that allow them the freedom and opportunity to explore adoption-related issues whenever they arise. This family environment begins from the moment the child is brought home.

THE SENSE OF SELF, THE GROWTH OF TRUST

All infants have a good deal of emotional growing to do. They must learn who they are, how they are distinct from others in the world, how to be curious and adventurous and yet safe and secure. According to Erik Erikson, the most important psychological task of early infancy is the development of a sense of trust, to which all these other goals are related.[2]

Trust allows an infant to feel he can depend on his own behavior as well as that of his caregivers. Without trust, he may grow up doubting his own self-worth, and doubting the motives of everyone he meets. But with trust, the baby can develop into a mature individual capable of giving and receiving love. Most parents, adoptive or biological, nurture this sense of trust by providing care with consistency and warmth.

Trusting another individual implies that a baby has a sense that he is distinct from other people. If the boundary between "I" and "not-I" doesn't exist, trust is not an issue. We used to think that it took many months for infants to start to understand that they were separate beings, but new research shows that the sense of the self, of being a distinct entity, begins from the moment of birth. Daniel Stern, a psychiatrist at Cornell University Medical Center, has categorized three components of the self that arise during the first ten months of life: the "emergent self," the "core self," and the "subjective self."[3]

The "sense of emergent self," according to Stern, is a purely sensorimotor way of experiencing the world. Starting at birth, the infant tries to make sense of his perceptions, motor actions, and primitive thoughts and emotions. This is an overwhelming task for a newborn; as Stern puts it, "the integrative networks that are forming are not yet embraced by a single organizing subjective perspective."

By two to six months, the infant begins to develop a "sense of core self." This is a physically based awareness that the baby is a separate being "with a unique [emotional] life and history that belong to it . . . [which] operates outside of awareness." Now infants start to sense that not only are their bodies separate from Mother, but so is everything else about themselves and their lives.

Between seven and nine months of age, a third component starts to develop: the "sense of subjective self." This is when the infant realizes that other minds exist, making him able to relate to other people's feelings, thoughts, and emotions. Now the infant can, at a primitive level, infer other people's mental states from the way they behave. As Stern writes, "Mental states between people can now be 'read,' matched, aligned with, or tuned to (or misread, mismatched, misaligned, or misattuned)." This helps explain the uncanny ability of babies to tune in to the moods, expressions, gestures, and tones of voice of the people they are with. They don't understand what they sense, because they have no words for it, but babies are often in touch with the emotional states of their loved ones—and their own gestures reveal this.

At around fifteen to eighteen months, the infant develops a fourth component of Stern's model, the "verbal sense of self." This allows for self-reflection and the beginnings of true comprehension of the self. The verbal sense of self is the one we are aware of most easily because it is represented through language and other accessible symbols. But even though it dominates, the earlier components of self (emergent, core, and subjective) continue to exist and to influence who we are. We will describe the sense of verbal self in the next chapter.

SETTING THE STAGE FOR ADOPTION ADJUSTMENT

Because trust develops so naturally in most homes, adopted and nonadopted infants tend to interact with their parents in much the same way. So it's easy for new adoptive parents to be lulled into the belief that being adopted won't make any difference to their children. This is a false belief; it *will* make a difference. Being adopted might not matter to babies in the first year or two of life, but it will matter eventually.

"Adoption is not identical with producing one's own child," writes Sanford N. Katz of the Boston College Law School. "It is raising and integrating another's biological child into one's own family. Not to recognize this reality is to romanticize adoption."[4]

During infancy, though, the differences between adoptive and biological families are subtle. Study after study has shown that adoptive parent-infant pairs look a lot like biological parent-infant pairs. They form "attachment" relationships, the underpinnings of all subsequent relationships, in ways that are virtually identical. Indeed, when we have studied babies who were adopted before the age of six months, we usually could not distinguish them from babies in biological families.[5]

The differences that do exist in these early months are historical —that is, in the way in which parents and baby came together, the context in which the family was built. Adopting a baby is vastly different from giving birth to a baby. Eventually, these differences will start to matter to the adoptive family.

Unlike the fixed nine-month span of a normal pregnancy, adoption can occur on a whimsical timetable. The time between "conception" (filing for adoption) and "delivery" (bringing home a baby) can range from a few weeks to six, seven, eight years or more. And even before the clock starts ticking, most adoptive parents have first had to wrestle with the problems, such as infertility, that led them to consider adoption in the first place.

"I felt like a failure," says our patient Cheryl, forty-two, about the period during her early thirties when she suffered through repeated miscarriages and one stillbirth. Now the mother of a six-year-old daughter who was adopted at birth, Cheryl still is haunted by the memory of those painful years:

"It was especially hard when I saw my sister producing like a veritable baby machine. All of my friends were parents. We were the only ones who had failed, or it seemed like that at least. I spent a lot of nights crying about it."

But the decision to adopt can often free infertile couples from the torment they had undergone in trying to conceive.

"Our infertility is in the past," says Marla, a thirty-two-year-old teacher, whose five years of treatment included surgery and fertility drugs. After her decision to adopt, she recalls, "We never went back to our infertility specialist, I never charted another month of temperatures, nor have I shed a tear at the onset of a new menstrual cycle. I have loaned out all my infertility literature and thrown out my years of temperature charts. I once read, 'You can clutch the past so tightly to your chest that it leaves your arms too full to embrace the present.' I believe this to be true."

Once they decide to adopt, couples usually feel an overwhelming relief and an eagerness to get on with the next stage of family life. But they have still more hurdles to leap over: doctors, lawyers, agencies, baby brokers, social workers, counselors, each with a new set of demands and distractions.

"I think I wanted it [adopting a baby] more than my husband did," Cheryl recalls. "He was ambivalent. He wasn't sure that he could accept another person's child."

And then there are the comments of others, callous or unthinking words from friends and relatives who truly consider adoption a second-class form of parenthood. They speak their minds, these friends and relatives, with comments like, "It's too bad you couldn't have a baby the regular way" or "If only you knew the joy that comes with having a baby of your own." They may even put adoptive parents on a tilted pedestal with backhanded compliments like, "Oh, you two are doing such a wonderful thing, raising someone else's baby."

"Family members continue to make comments that sometimes bother me," Marla says.

She remembers the stab she felt when her father-in-law introduced her son to an acquaintance with, "This is my grandson. He's adopted." Relatives also say things to Marla like, "I wonder whose temperament he inherited" or "Watch, now you'll get pregnant and have one of your own."

The worst comment, Marla says, came when she was in a store with her son, who was about a year old at the time:

"I ran into a man I served on the parish council with (father of five). He asked how everything was going and I said something like, 'He's into everything now that he's walking.' His response (said laughingly): 'Well, it's too late to send him back now!' If I could have spit fire I would have!"

Judy says that when her family found out she was adopting a baby from Brazil, they were very concerned about the child's skin color. The unspoken message, of course, was, "Will he be like us?" The irony of this, Judy says, is that her adoption lawyer kept offering her and her husband the kind of babies he thought American couples wanted —blond and blue-eyed—when in fact she and her husband were dark and olive-skinned, and such a child would have looked more out of place in their family than a typical Brazilian baby.

When Scott was about six months old, Judy found out, to her great surprise, that she was pregnant. Her biological son, Kevin, is just fifteen months younger than Scott. That is when the comments began.

"I noticed some prejudice against adopted children when Kevin was born," Judy recalls. "People would make some comments like, 'Oh, it's so nice to have a child of your own' or 'You must be so happy to give birth to your own child.' I've since had relatives ask me about my adopted son's intelligence—he's six now—but no one asks me about the biological child's intelligence."

Some friends and relatives, of course, give little thought to the adoptive status of the children in their circle; they just embrace their new nieces, nephews, or grandchildren without hesitation. "My parents just think of my children as theirs, just like any other grandchildren," says one adoptive mother.

But the history of many adoptive parents—which includes infertility, the uncertainty of the adoption process, the intrusion of being observed during a home study, and the stinging comments of others —can undermine their sense of confidence in their parenting skills. Some may respond by feeling less than capable of caring for their children, even long after the children have arrived. Their sense of "entitlement"—their feeling that they deserve to be parents—may be compromised. When the parents are unnerved in this way, their heightened anxiety can create a home environment that compromises the development of the infant's sense of trust. Fortunately, this doesn't happen in most adoptive families. In fact, most families leap the hurdles put in their way with relative ease.

A Word About Bonding

Lending credibility to the general, though unspoken, feeling that adoptive parents aren't the same as "real" parents is a new field of scientific study that has emerged in the past decade: the study of "bonding." According to pop psychologists, the bonding between parent and child begins during pregnancy, is heightened when a mother sees a sonogram of her fetus, and is cemented as the fetus "eavesdrops" on the sounds of mother's and father's voices.

One mail-order catalog catering to yuppie parents is trying to cash in on this popular notion that a good relationship starts with intrauterine bonding. For fifty-nine dollars plus postage, expectant parents can receive a contraption that straps around the pregnant mother's belly, attaches to a microphone, and supposedly allows mother, father, or sibling to speak directly into a device that amplifies the voice inside the womb. This way, reads the catalog text, the fetus can hear better and, theoretically, bond better.

But as we shall see, true attachment to a primary caretaker, the kind that lasts a lifetime, doesn't happen in utero or in the first moments after delivery. It is something that grows slowly, over weeks, months, and even years of loving interaction, and it can grow just as well between a parent and infant who are not biologically connected as between a parent and infant who are.

What clinicians and researchers look for in attachment relationships is not the same as what happens during "bonding," a notion that came into vogue in the late 1970s after the work of two Cleveland pediatricians, Marshall Klaus and John Kennel.[6] Bonding is said to occur in the first hours, or at most days, after birth, when both mother and newborn are biologically primed to connect. In the popular view of bonding, the mother's hormones are set up to make her fall in love with the baby; the baby is alert and ready to respond soon after his trip down the birth canal. Attachment, on the other hand, is an emotional relationship that develops gradually, after weeks and months of daily contact, conversation, caregiving, and cuddling.

The notion of the "bonding hour" has had some benefits and some drawbacks. On the plus side, it has forced many hospitals to allow the new family to spend time together in the recovery room immediately after birth, and to allow for "rooming in" on the maternity ward. Until relatively recently, most hospitals simply whisked away the infant to the nursery as soon as he was delivered, weighed, and measured.

But on the minus side, the "bonding hour" has made parents who couldn't cuddle their babies in the recovery room—either because mother or baby was too sick or because the baby was adopted—feel they have missed out on something that can never be retrieved. If they did not have that time together, some new parents believe, they will forever be hampered in their relationship to their babies.

The fact is that while many lower animals do indeed show a biologically based bonding during critical periods soon after birth, the scientific evidence for such bonding in human infants is weak. The bonding, or "imprinting," of animals explains experiments such as those of the famous "Papa Goose"—Konrad Lorenz, the Austrian ethologist (student of animal behavior) who developed a motherlike relationship with a group of goslings because he made himself be the first object they saw after they hatched.[7] "Papa Goose" captured the public and professional imagination in part because his experiment yielded such a lively visual result: a long string of cackling geese following the white-haired scientist everywhere, apparently thinking he was their mother.

But human infants are not geese. They do not emerge from the uterus bonded or attached to their biological parents, nor do they look around and say "Mama!" to the first person visible. This is not to deny the well-documented capabilities of newborns. In the past fifteen years, researchers have uncovered previously unrecognized skills and sensitivities of infants just hours or days old. Jean MacFarlane of the University of California at Berkeley, for instance, showed that three-day-old infants were capable of differentiating their own mother's milk from that of another nursing woman.[8] She placed babies on their backs and presented them with breast pads saturated with milk from their own mother and another, one on each side of their heads. They most often turned toward the pad with their own mother's milk.

But recognition is not attachment. Babies are born with a built-in set of response capabilities and signaling systems, but it is only after a long period of using them that true attachment develops. These capabilities—crying, smiling, vocalizing, sucking, gazing, head-turning—will promote close interaction between caregiver and baby; eventually, this will lead to a two-way emotional bond.

The key word here is "eventually." It takes weeks and weeks for an infant to form a solid emotional attachment with anyone.

ATTACHMENT: THE ESSENTIAL BOND

Here is how the process works. When a newborn cries, mother or father feeds or diapers or picks up the baby. When a newborn smiles, mother or father smiles back. When a newborn vocalizes, mother or father vocalizes back, using many of the pauses, facial expressions, and changes in inflection that are used in normal conversations.

Any mother or father—indeed, any adult who spends a concentrated amount of time with the newborn—will behave in much the same way. After a few weeks, parent and baby have choreographed a little dance, a synchrony in their responses to one another. This dance can be done with any caregiver who responds sensitively to the young infant's cues.

Only later, after the age of four to six months, does the baby seem to prefer Mother (or other significant caretaker) to anyone else, especially in times of stress. This is the key to our notion of attachment: the baby seeks out the attachment figure as a source of comfort when he is upset. And for babies who were adopted in the first month or so of life, "Mother" is defined not as the woman whose voice was overheard in the womb, but as the woman who did all the responding and diapering and feeding and cooing—the adoptive mother.

We should note that the word "Mother" is being used as a shorthand for any significant attachment figure. Infants are capable of forming attachments to many figures—mother, father, nanny, grandparent, sibling—but these attachments don't usually form with the same intensity, nor do they serve the same purpose for the infant.

Babies of this age also are clear in their preference for members of their immediate family over friends and relatives they don't know as well.

"It felt as though it was meant to be," says Jeanne about the first months of life with her adopted daughter. "It's as if God had us in mind when she was born."

Jeanne's daughter, Sarah, was a "securely attached" infant, the type first described by the noted British psychiatrist John Bowlby in 1969.[9] According to Bowlby, secure attachments early in life are good predictors of emotional health later in life. By the same token, insecure attachments early in life could presage later difficulties, such as problems forming relationships, personality disorders, and feelings of insecurity or low self-esteem.

Bowlby described a securely attached infant as one who "uses mother as a base, keeps notes of her whereabouts, and exchanges glances with her [while exploring a new environment]. From time to time he returns to her and enjoys contact with her. When she returns after a brief absence he greets her warmly."[10]

A controversial experiment to measure how well mother and infant are attached was developed by a protégé of Bowlby's, psychologist Mary Ainsworth of the University of Virginia. She and her colleagues devised a twenty-minute laboratory scenario involving mother-infant pairs called the Strange Situation.[11] First mother and infant are alone in a room, observed through a one-way mirror. Then a female stranger comes in and converses with Mother. Mother leaves, and stranger tries to play with Baby. Mother returns, Stranger leaves, Mother leaves. Baby is alone for a while, Stranger comes back, and finally Mother comes back and Stranger leaves for good.

The way the infant greets Mother during the reunion periods, particularly the last reunion, reveals how well or how poorly the two are attached. Most infants—about 75 percent in Ainsworth's early experiments—exhibit "secure attachment." They usually continue to play and explore when the parent is out of the room, either alone or in the stranger's presence, but when Mother comes back they make contact with her. Securely attached infants, during the last reunion, look at Mother, vocalize to her, or, if they were distressed in her absence, seek contact and comfort from her.

Ainsworth also identified two forms of insecure attachment: "avoidant attachment" and "resistant attachment."[12] Avoidant attachment reflects some difficulty between parent and child. The infant seems to ignore Mother, even when she is in the room, and does not use her as a base for exploration. The baby hardly seems to notice when Mother leaves, and hardly seems to notice when she returns. He is just as easily comforted by a stranger as by his own parent.

Resistant attachment, on the other hand, is shown when the infant is distressed or anxious even when Mother is in the room, and has trouble using her as a secure base for exploration. During the last reunion, the infant shows two conflicting types of responses, almost simultaneously: he seeks contact with her, clings to her, yet seems to find no comfort in Mother's arms; indeed, the baby almost appears to be angry with her. This type of insecure attachment reflects not only difficulty but ambivalence in the parent-child relationship. It seems to be the category most predictive of problems later on.[13]

A secure relationship with Mother—or some other important attachment figure—allows a baby to get through periods of stress. With this person available as a secure base, a baby under stress, such as the infant in the Strange Situation, can still be independent, free to explore or play, secure in the knowledge that the caregiver is nearby and available as a source of security, comfort, and confidence. This translates in later years into greater sociability, maturity, and ability to form intimate relationships.

The Strange Situation has been criticized as failing to measure what it claims to measure. Some critics say the baby's reaction to this experimental situation is more a reflection of his temperament, his innate ability to deal with novelty, than of the relationship between parent and child.

But the elevated place of this research tool in the psychological literature does reveal one thing: the professional consensus that the early relationship to Mother is significant far beyond infancy.

Behavior during the Strange Situation has been recorded for adopted infants and compared to behavior of nonadopted infants.[14] As far as quality of attachment is concerned, adopted mother-infant pairs tend to look almost exactly like biological pairs. The only differences that have been noted have occurred in infants adopted after the age of about six months. Since these babies have usually already formed an attachment with their biological or foster parents, they come to the adoptive parents following a disruption of a previous relationship, which often leads to a sense of loss and emotional or behavioral disorganization.[15]

When babies have already attached to a birth mother or foster mother, they are likely to come into the adoptive home already grieving for that primary bond. And because they are preverbal, their grieving can look like other problems, usually physical, that cause the adoptive parents great anxiety.

Justin Call, a psychiatrist at the University of California at Irvine, has developed a chart of the ups and downs of adjustment problems in an adopted infant's responses to moving to a new home (Table 2). Signs of distress show up to a greater or lesser extent at certain vulnerable stages, and even the signs themselves are different depending on how old the infant is. In the first six months of life, distress reveals itself as trouble with sleeping or eating—refusal to eat, spitting up, chronic diarrhea, difficulty sleeping for extended stretches—or as irritability, crying for no apparent reason, or, in the most extreme cases, as failure to thrive.

In the second six months, distress is signified in more sophisticated ways. The baby might exhibit searching behavior, as though looking for his previous caretaker; uncontrollable crying; withdrawal; uninterest in playing or eating; clinging behavior; lack of vitality; frequent illnesses and accidents; weight loss; or even facial and body expressions that indicate sadness.

Table 2 Responses to a New Home[16]

Birth to four weeks	Little distress seen; newborns are focused on having body needs met, not attentive to surroundings
Four to twelve weeks	Much distress seen; infants can respond to new stimuli in the environment, cannot shut it out when it becomes too much
Twelve to twenty-four weeks	Little distress seen; babies can respond to more complex stimuli, modify it as needed, adjust better to changes in diet and environment
Six to twelve months	Much distress seen; babies are grieving for loss of the primary caretaker, to whom attachment is intense at this age

But for all the possible problems in getting used to their new adoptive home, we hasten to point out that children tend to be incredibly resilient. If they weren't, then virtually every child adopted from a foreign country, indeed every child adopted after any transitional foster care, would be a child at considerable risk. But in fact the evidence suggests that the great majority of these children adjust quite normally.

Because many infant adoptions are not legally finalized for at least six months—sometimes longer—adoptive families have an additional barrier set up in the task of bonding with their babies. Some adoptive parents, albeit a small minority, keep at emotional arm's length until the adoption is finalized, so they won't get hurt if something goes wrong. The recent film *Immediate Family* and a segment of the television show "L.A. Law" have popularized this notion that birth mothers often change their minds and want their babies back. When parents hold back emotionally, they can create a home environment that undermines the development of their baby's sense of trust.

THE VAGARIES OF TEMPERAMENT

Listen to the way people talk about babies: "He is a difficult baby" or "She always wants her own way"; "She has always been so sweet-natured" or "He never has any trouble sleeping." These comments reveal the general belief that babies come to us with their personalities intact, already true to the type of person each will eventually become.

Psychologists call this inborn personality a newborn's "temperament." New York University psychiatrists Alexander Thomas and Stella Chess, two leading researchers in the field, have identified nine dimensions of infant temperament: activity level; regularity in sleeping, eating, and eliminating; response to new stimulation (approach or withdrawal); adaptability; intensity of reaction; threshold of responsiveness; quality of mood (pleasant or unpleasant); distractibility; and attention span or persistence.[17]

Investigators categorize infant temperament because it can say so much about the parent-child relationship. If the newborn's temperament fits into the parents' personalities and lifestyle, and meets their expectations, the attachment between parents and child is likely to work well; if the "fit" is poor, the relationship may be poor.

Frank Mills and Elaine Conners are two busy, ambitious lawyers who are easily riled and always running half an hour late. Elaine got pregnant in her late thirties, at the peak of her legal career. Her little boy, Jared Conners-Mills, turned out to be a "difficult" baby. Jared had irregular eating and sleeping patterns, intense reactions, and trouble adjusting to changes or to new people. What babies like Jared most need is a calm environment, a predictable schedule, patient caregiving —things that Frank and Elaine just were not capable of providing. Jared grew more and more demanding, and Frank and Elaine grew more and more disappointed at having a son who was so irritable and at times downright unappealing.

Clearly, even in biological families like Jared's, poor fits between parents and baby simply happen. But in adoptive families, poor fits may be more likely. To the extent that temperament runs in the family, the lack of a biological tie may make it more likely for an adopted baby to be quite different from his parents. Quiet, reserved parents may end up with an active, fussy baby they cannot relate to; affectionate, playful parents may end up with a baby who is withdrawn and doesn't like to be cuddled. When the fit is poor, the attachment may be more difficult.

"He's so fussy, he cries a lot, he doesn't sleep well at night," said a patient of ours about her adopted baby when he was twelve months old. "You can't believe how tired I get from that. I expected he would be easier to care for, like my sister's baby."

In adoptive families, it may actually be harder to cope with a poor fit. When a "difficult child" is brought home in a biological family, there's often the comfort of Grandma coming for a visit and telling Mother, "You had colic, too, when I brought you home from the hospital, but by three months you grew out of it." In adoptive families, if such assurances are made, they might seem no more relevant than comments made by a visiting friend. Remarks on the order of "My children were like that, too" are helpful, but they don't resonate in the same way that family legacies resonate. They don't carry the weight of genetics, the impression that a baby's sweet or difficult nature is part of what has been passed on through the generations.

Complicating the picture of an adoptee's temperament are the problems associated with being the product of a high-stress pregnancy. The intrauterine environment for many adopted children might have been one in which the birth mother was casual about using cigarettes or alcohol or drugs, failed to get prenatal care, or was herself still a growing child—any one of which can adversely affect a fetus's physical and neurological development.

In addition, whatever personality traits led the birth parents to the pregnancy in the first place—impulsiveness, immaturity, poor judgment—may themselves have a genetic component, which could get passed on to the child. Although research has not indicated any increased vulnerability for adoptees during infancy, this genetic and prenatal legacy could help explain the increased problems in psychological adjustment later in childhood—increased aggressiveness, oppositional behavior, impulsiveness, hyperactivity.

The interactions between baby and parent in the very first few days of life might also help shape a baby's temperament. If a parent is relaxed and calm, even a jittery baby might be settled early on, and certain inborn traits that might eventually produce a "difficult baby" may be smoothed away.

A Different Style of Family Building

Just how different *is* an adoptive family from a nonadoptive one? When do the differences emerge? And how important are they? The way in which parents answer these questions, it turns out, helps determine how comfortable both the parents and the children are about the adoption.

Twenty-five years ago, the Canadian sociologist H. David Kirk noticed that there were essentially two types of adoptive families: those that felt themselves to be identical *in every way* to biological families, and those that acknowledged and accepted differences between their own families and biological families.[18] He called the two styles "rejection of differences" and "acknowledgment of differences." We have added a third type, "insistence on differences," to describe the family that not only recognizes the differences inherent in adoption, but emphasizes them and blames many normal family events on them.[19]

It is easy to see from Kirk's choice of terminology that the strategy he considers most constructive is the one that acknowledges and accepts the differences between adoptive and nonadoptive families. So do many other adoption experts—ourselves included. "Adoption in America has been based on the ancient Roman ideal of imitating nature," writes Boston lawyer Sanford N. Katz. "The popular practice of maintaining a certain age differentiation between adopters and adoptees, matching complexions, hair and eye colorations, body structures, national origin, and even religion, derives from this antiquated Roman goal."[20]

But adopting a baby is not the same as giving birth to a baby, and the pretense of the family being "just like any other family" can be damaging to all concerned.

Our patient Carole exhibited the destructive effect of the "rejection of differences" style of adoptive parenting. We met Carole while she was in a deep depression after attending an adoptive parents' support-group meeting—though how she ended up at the meeting is a mystery, since Carole never defined herself as an adoptive parent. After nearly nine years of trying to have a baby of her own—including four years of infertility testing and treatment—Carole had adopted a nine-month-old baby she named Jennifer. At first, she refused to acknowledge that her daughter was adopted. She told a few of her closest friends, but when she talked to acquaintances she was careful to leave the impression that Jennifer was her biological child.

This subterfuge could be accounted for by a family legend with which Carole was raised: the myth of matriarchy. Carole's grandmother was extremely close to Carole's great-grandmother; her mother was extremely close to her grandmother; and Carole was extremely close to her mother and grandmother. Carole had always expected to have a little girl of her own to follow in this family tradition.

"What will my mother and my grandmother say?" Carole wondered when she faced her infertility. "I've let them down. I'll never be able to carry on the strong maternal line if I can't have my own child."

Because motherhood was so important in Carole's family, accepting her own infertility was a deep blow to Carole's ego. She felt less than adequate, viewed her body as betraying her, saw herself as defective. Never having come fully to terms with her infertility, she could not come to terms with her status as an adoptive mother. She thought that if she pretended Jennifer were her biological child, that would make things better—and would make her mother and grandmother accept the baby more easily.

But Carole is unusual. Most adoptive mothers and fathers adjust very well to parenthood, in many cases even better than the average biological parent—precisely because they have had to confront so many tragedies along the way. They are coming from a state they experienced as one of deprivation—that is, childlessness in the face of infertility. Having a baby relieves this deprivation.

In an adoptive family, the new baby is desperately wanted, and the parents have a remarkable set of skills with which to deal with him. Adoptive parents are usually more mature than biological parents, more stable in their marriage (after all, it's weathered quite a few rough times already), more financially secure, and more adept at coping with stress.

In 1982, psychologist Janet L. Hoopes of Bryn Mawr College published a long-term study that compared the parenting styles and family dynamics of fifty-four families, half of them adoptive and half not.[21] She rated adoptive mothers higher than any other group of parents—higher than adoptive fathers, biological mothers, or biological fathers—on measures of parent-child relatedness, acceptance of the child, praising of the child, affection and warmth, and handling the child.

That is the good news. The bad news is perhaps the inevitable flip side of this intense gratitude for the adopted child: adoptive mothers were more protective, more anxious, more likely to foster dependency, and less likely to be egalitarian (allowing for individual points of view) in the raising of their children.

Overall, however, the parents who seemed most competent in Hoopes's investigation were the adoptive parents. As a group, she found, they were less intrusive, less controlling, and less authoritarian than nonadoptive parents. And during their children's infancy and preschool years, times of great stress in any marriage, adoptive couples were less likely than were new biological parents to have conflicts in their relationships. This may be partly because adoptive parents have usually been married for a long time before their babies arrive—an average of 10.5 years, compared to just 2.5 years for biological parents.[22]

David Kirk's classic book about adoption, *Shared Fate*, offers a point of view that can explain why the bond between adopted child and adoptive parent can be so strong. According to Kirk, they all have suffered a deep sense of loss: the parents through the loss of the ability to bear their own biological children, the children through the loss of their birth parents. When the adoptive parents understand the shared nature of their losses, says Kirk, they can be more empathetic toward the child and better able to raise him in a sensitive and understanding way.

"The parents' recall of their own deprivation and pain, worked through but not discarded, may provide an instrument for keeping open the channels of communication," Kirk writes. "Through such means they may be able to apprehend the occasions when the child seeks information and support."[23]

Family life is the bedrock from which personality develops; it is the foundation for subsequent adjustment to adoption. Now that we have looked at this foundation, we can start down the developmental path along with the growing child. Soon he will begin to understand one basic fact of his own life: that he is adopted.

Chapter 2

TODDLERHOOD AND PRESCHOOL

AGES ONE TO FIVE

The earliest memory I have of my adoption is before I began kindergarten. I was in my grandmother's bedroom, upstairs, looking outside at the neighbor's house. A girl one year older than I lived there. My mother came up behind me, looking outside also, and said, "See Barbara? They had to take her. But we picked you out special."

Special. This label haunted me. What did I do to be special? If I stop being special, will I be sent back? Where's "back," anyway? I don't feel special—I don't feel any better than any other kids. In fact, I often feel worse. Why didn't my mother keep me, like all the other kids' mothers? What's wrong with me that she gave me away?

—*Kate, age twenty-nine,*
adopted at four days old

Toddlerhood has its beginnings with the so-called "first adolescence"—a term whose accuracy will be confirmed by any parent with a child in the Terrible Twos. A toddler's favorite words are "no" and "mine"; a preschooler's favorite concept is "I can do it all by myself." The young child is now developing a stronger sense of self, a growing independence, an autonomy that will allow her to become a self-sufficient human being.

During toddlerhood, roughly ages one through three, children are furiously busy gaining control of themselves and of the world. Physically, real control begins during this stage—control over their bowel

43

and bladder functions, control over their movement through walking and running, control over their growth through the ability to feed themselves, control over their parents through their "no's," their tantrums, and their ability to run away when they are truly displeased.

By the preschool period, ages three through about five, a child is getting ready for the next step: to head out into the world and knock 'em dead. She's beginning to develop the ability to explore, to initiate projects, and to question everything she sees. She's mastered skills that will take her places—tying her shoes, fetching her coat, riding her tricycle. All these skills help her as she continues to separate from her parents, getting ready to venture forth from the security of home into the wild and exciting unknown beyond the front door.

And as she heads out into that unknown world, she will begin to confront the fact of her own adoption.

THE "VERBAL SELF" DEVELOPS

Until toddlerhood, babies don't know quite who they are. Show a baby her reflection in the mirror, and she'll think it's another baby. We know this because of the work of psychological researchers who came up with a clever way of demonstrating what a baby thinks she's seeing—by putting an orange dot on the baby's nose.[1]

In these studies, when young babies were shown their reflections and noticed the orange dot, they tried to touch the nose in the mirror. But by about the age of eighteen months, something happened. When toddlers were shown their orange-nosed reflections, they tried to touch their own noses. They had learned that the babies in the mirrors were their own reflections—and that if the mirror-babies' noses were orange, their own noses must be, too.

Now, at the age of fifteen to eighteen months, toddlers start developing what Daniel Stern of Cornell calls the "verbal sense of self." As the child gains language, she is able "to objectify the self, to be self-reflective, to comprehend."[2] Words bring with them the ability to think about the self on a new, more representational level, an ability that becomes elaborated over the course of development.

The verbal sense of self is the one we are aware of most easily because it is represented through our language and other symbol systems. But even though it is the component of self brought most easily to the fore, the earlier components of self that developed during infancy (the emergent self, the core self, and the subjective self) continue to exist and influence who we are.

One way to measure the toddler's developing sense of self is to listen to her choice of words. During the second year of life, there is a sharp change in the use of the personal pronouns "I," "my," "mine," and "me." A fourteen-month-old may climb up a chair and say merely "Up." A twenty-month-old will add the personal pronoun: "Me up." Scientists at Harvard University have actually counted children's use of pronouns, and they noted a significant increase in the use of "me" words beginning at about the age of nineteen months.[3]

Later, the notion of the self becomes even more refined. At about the age of three, a child can define herself primarily in terms of her activities. Ask a toddler who she is and she will say, "I sleep in a bunk bed," "I Mommy's baby," or "I go to day care." Within a few years, this self-definition becomes more abstract, incorporating qualities that are innate and unique to the individual. A five-year-old's self-description might be something like "I am happy" or "I am smart."

BECOMING A PERSON

As a toddler develops a sense of self, her crucial psychological task is to set that self apart from all others. The ultimate goal is to become autonomous—or, as clinicians put it, to "individuate."

It's not an easy job. In order to become an independent person, a toddler first must realize that part of the world exists without her. For there to be an "I," there first must be a "not-I." And as we saw in the previous chapter, this realization does not occur until midway through the first year of life. Until then, the infant considers the boundary between herself and the rest of the world totally porous; there is no difference between herself and her mother, her own body and her father's, her needs and the needs of whoever it is who is meeting those needs.

Gradually, though, this boundary develops. Some researchers say the process starts as early as the age of five months, when infants first recognize that they and their mothers are two distinct people—a kind of second birth experience. Gradually, between about five months and fifteen months, babies assert their independence and willingness to explore and experiment. But for a short while, between about fifteen and twenty-two months, even apparently independent babies seem to regress, becoming more clingy and dependent for a while.[4] What's going through the baby's mind, we expect, is something along the lines of, "Do I really want to go out there totally on my own?" or "Will Mother always be here even after I become a fully independent child?"

Erik Erikson considers this period to be critical for the development of a child's sense of self. He divides it into two phases. The "autonomy versus shame and doubt" phase, lasting from about age one and a half to three, involves a psychological focus on establishing independence. The "initiative versus guilt" phase, ages three to six, focuses on a related task, the development of skills needed for self-care.[5]

In Erikson's analysis, toddlers must be allowed to do what they are capable of doing, without having too much or too little expected of them, in order to develop a sense of competence, independence, and self-esteem—the ingredients required for autonomy. And preschoolers must be given a clear understanding of rules and expectations in order to develop the freedom that comes with having reasonable limits. These rules can help young children internalize a sense of right and wrong, and within that context they can allow themselves to be enthusiastic, self-motivated, and adventurous.

It's easy to see, in the "initiative versus guilt" stage, how these two issues can be in conflict for a young child. Imagine four-year-old Miles coming home from nursery school with a painting that his mother praises lavishly. The next weekend, he decides to wake up early and do something entirely on his own that his mother is sure to like. He paints the same design again—this time on his bedroom wall. Now, though, his mother has no praise, only sharp comments like, "What's the matter with you? Don't you know you're not supposed to paint on the walls?" Miles is left with no sense of accomplishment, only a sense of guilt, and he is punished for disobeying a rule he didn't even know existed.

Guilt in small doses is okay, Erikson says; in fact, it's necessary. A sense of guilt is what helps a child gain self-control over her future actions. But too much criticism from parents can stifle a child's sense of initiative and cripple her with guilt. What is needed are some clear rules for self-expression—rules that many preschools and kindergartens lay out early and often, but rules that many households fail to state explicitly.

BECOMING A THINKER

Among the important life skills developed during the toddler and preschool years is the ability to think symbolically. With the emergence of language and other forms of symbolization—gesturing, drawing, mental imagery—children begin to break out of their restricted view of the world by mentally representing the people, objects, and events around them. This capability allows children to think about their world without having to act on it with their senses. For the infant, Mother is someone who is felt, seen, heard, and tasted, whereas for the older child she is someone who can be represented in language, drawing, symbolic play, or as an internal mental picture.

Much of what we know about the development of reasoning, or cognition, came originally from the careful work of Jean Piaget, the Swiss psychologist, biologist, and philosopher. Beginning in the 1920s, Piaget spent decades observing and testing the thinking abilities of his own three children and others in the community. Out of these observations came an elaborate theory of cognitive development. Succeeding generations of developmental researchers have refined Piaget's theory. Nevertheless, our current knowledge of young children's thinking owes much to the insights of this remarkable man.[6]

According to Piaget, the child between the ages of two and five is a "preoperational" thinker. This means the child is able to make cause-and-effect leaps but cannot really perform the mental "operations" required for true logic. The preschooler's thinking ability is constrained by her egocentricity, her utter conviction that the world revolves around her and her needs.

We recently saw a four-year-old girl, Lorie, who was experiencing great separation anxiety. In the course of therapy it emerged that Lorie previously had been quite angry at her mother for punishing her. In her mind, Lorie said, she had thought "terrible" things about her mother and wished she were dead. Coincidentally, Lorie's mother was suddenly taken ill and had to be hospitalized for several weeks. Lorie came to believe that she had caused her mother's illness by her terrible thoughts. In her effort to undo her misdeed, and to ward off the possibility of abandonment, Lorie now would not allow her mother to leave her sight.

Preoperational thinking is a familiar mode to anyone who has spent any time with a young child. A child's leaps of logic usually sound rational, but on closer inspection they are not. The perplexing thought process of Winnie-the-Pooh, the beloved bear from A. A. Milne's children's books, is a perfect example of preoperational thinking.

Here is an example: Pooh hears a loud buzzing sound coming from the top of a large oak tree in the forest, and he tries to figure out what the noise can signify.

"That buzzing-noise means something. You don't get a buzzing-noise like that, just buzzing and buzzing, without its meaning something. If there's a buzzing-noise, somebody's making a buzzing-noise, and the only reason for making a buzzing-noise that I know of is because you're a bee."

Then he thought another long time, and said: "And the only reason for being a bee that I know of is making honey." And then he got up, and said: "And the only reason for making honey is so as I can eat it." So he began to climb the tree.[7]

A preschooler is not only an egocentric thinker, but he is usually quite literal. The actor Fred Gwynne has made clever use of this literalness in his books for children, *A Chocolate Moose for Dinner* and *The King Who Rained*. The misspellings in the titles are a clue to what the books are like. When Gwynne's five-year-old heroine says, "Daddy says there should be more car pools," her perplexity is illustrated with a picture of a group of automobiles in bathing suits lounging around a swimming pool.

Young children don't understand metaphors, or puns, or even homonyms (two words that sound alike but mean different things, like "moose" and "mousse"). Their literal interpretations can have funny, or sometimes not so funny, consequences in children who are told important things.

Because five-year-olds *seem* so rational, parents believe they have really heard and understood their explanations about what happened to Grandma when she died, or how babies are born, or that they are adopted. But this isn't always the case.

Three-and-a-half-year-old Melissa was terribly anxious about going to her grandmother's house, a visit she had always looked forward to with glee. It turned out that Melissa had just overheard her mother telling someone that Grandma had recently dyed her hair—and she dreaded seeing her beloved grandmother with dead hair.

Similarly, when Matthew was just shy of four, he set out one day scouring the house for something. He looked behind chairs, in wastepaper baskets, in bookcases. Finally his mother asked him what he was doing. "I'm looking for Daddy's mind," Matthew said. The night before, Matthew's parents had argued, and Matthew had formed his odd impression when he heard his mother exclaim, "I think you've lost your mind!"

By the end of the preschool years, a young child is beginning to grow more comfortable with the signs and symbols that characterize a more mature thinking style. Signs are representations that are recognized by everyone in a society, such as the letters of the alphabet or the notes of a musical staff. Symbols are mental images of an individual's own construction. They have a private meaning, not necessarily one shared by anyone else.

Symbolic functioning is at work when four-year-old Samantha and Emily play "dress-up." A gold-colored scarf tied around Samantha's head represents a crown, another scarf around her neck a royal robe, and a stick from the backyard the scepter. Samantha is the princess, and Emily—wearing a cast-off black velvet jacket—is the prince. With carefully placed props, the girls have created a representation of a palace and its lavish gardens. When they take Samantha's mother on a tour of the grounds, though, all she sees is a backyard littered with toys! This type of imaginary play is an important stage in the development of symbolic thought, the precursor of true logic.

"I'M A DOPTED"—PARROTING THE ADOPTION STORY

Because a young child's thinking ability is so rudimentary, she generally has trouble understanding the full implications of being adopted. The advice of most adoption experts is to start talking to children about being adopted during toddlerhood, before they have a chance to develop their own ideas about adoption. Most parents dutifully follow this advice. But our research suggests that most children haven't the foggiest idea what Mom and Dad are talking about.[8]

"My father's a dentist, my mother's a teacher, and I'm a dopted," says a boy of five.

"Everybody's adopted, right?" a four-year-old girl will say.

One young woman remembers the exact evening when her aural confusion over what "adoption" meant began.

"I was marching around in my big sister's Brownie dress (I must have been three or four). I was pretending to be a "big girl" like Kimberly, my sister (older by five years), who proceeded to get angry at me for wearing her prized uniform. I refused to shed the garment, even come bathtime. The episode resulted in some harsh words from Mom who then dumped me—Brownie dress and all— into the tub. After the fight and a bath, I recall my mother drying me off with a towel. Then she told me that she "dropped" me. Throughout my childhood I mused over my gross interpretation of 'adopted' for 'dropped.' "

The words are often heard and often repeated, but to these children their meaning is still, quite obviously, vague.

Molly thought that being adopted meant being born—and vice versa. When she was five, her favorite game was to crawl under her mother's skirt, slither out, and yell, "I'm adopted now!"

But even though they don't quite understand the words used, most very young adoptees love their adoption stories. How could a young child help but love a story that's told over and over again, while she's cuddled in the arms of a parent speaking in loving tones, about the most important character in the world—her very own self? This sets up most young children to have warm and cozy feelings about being adopted. Still, no matter how often the story is repeated, no matter how fondly it's remembered, the meaning is probably not really sinking in yet.

Heather's parents always read a book to her at bedtime, but often instead of a book Heather wanted them to "Tell story"—talk about the day Heather was adopted. The story was always the same: how the parents went to the newborn nursery and picked Heather out of all the other children to be their own special baby. Every night Heather asked her parents to "Tell story," and every night the story was virtually the same.

When Heather was four, the family dog gave birth—with Heather and her parents watching in fascination—to seven puppies. That night at bedtime, Heather interrupted the adoption story with a question.

"I came from your tummy, didn't I?" Heather asked. Her mother looked at the child sitting on her lap and said, calmly, "No. Don't you remember we told you that another wonderful lady gave birth to you? Then we adopted you, just like other families are going to adopt Daisy's puppies." Heather became silent, sucked her thumb intensely, and shook her head. She looked distressed. "You never told me that, ever," she said solemnly.

Parents have been surprised by the way a seemingly straightforward explanation, or even an innocuous turn of phrase, is twisted in the confused mind of a five-year-old, who has no context in which to place the story of her birth.

Similarly, Jenna thought "adopted" was just another word for "born." Like many other adoptive parents, Jenna's were uncomfortable about the birth part of the "chosen child" story, so they just left it out. That's why, when Jenna was four years old, she answered our questions this way:

INTERVIEWER: Tell me, what does it mean to be adopted? What is adoption?

JENNA: It's like when you are small and you come home from the hospital.

I: Tell me more about that. Exactly what happens in adoption?

JENNA: The doctor takes the baby out of the mommy and
                then they take the baby home.
INTERVIEWER: Who takes the baby home?
J: The mommy and daddy . . . First the mommy
                pushes the baby out of her and then she takes it
                home . . . The daddy takes it, too.
I: And what's that called?
J: What you asked . . . adoption.

Andrew, who was also four, thought everybody was adopted. His
conversation with an interviewer went like this:

INTERVIEWER: What I want to ask you about is adoption. Have
                you heard that word before?
ANDREW: Sure. I'm adopted.
I: What does that mean? What's adoption mean?
A: Well mommy told me that when I was a baby I
                came out of another lady . . . she made me. After
                I was born, my mommy and daddy came and got
                me and took me home.
I: So first you came out of one lady and then you went
                home with another lady, your mommy . . . and of
                course your daddy too.
A: Yep. That's how it happens.
I: Is there any other way that grown-ups can become
                parents besides adopting a child?
A: What do you mean?
I: How do grown-ups become parents? How do they
                become a mommy or daddy?
A: They get a child . . . adopt him.
I: Is there any other way of becoming a mommy or
                daddy?
A: [Shakes head no.]
I: Do all kids come into their families after they are
                adopted?
A: Yep . . . That's the way they do it.

When asked if that meant that all kids are adopted, Andrew nodded
his head yes.
    When young children don't understand all the details of what it

means to be adopted, they may use their fertile imaginations to help fill in the blanks. That is what happened with Scott, who was adopted from Colombia at the age of two months. When Scott was about five, his parents started interviewing nannies to replace the babysitter they had brought from Colombia when Scott came to their home. "Scott said he wanted someone from Colombia," recalls his mother. She took this to be a healthy sign. But shortly afterward, Scott told her not to tell anyone where he was from.

"Imagining this was some adoption crisis and wondering what to do about it, I managed to calmly ask him what he wanted me to tell people," his mother says. "His reply was, 'Tell them I'm from outer space.' "

Some innocent details of the adoption story can also be misconstrued by the youngster and become the source of fears or insecurities. Susanna, now forty-four, was told during her early childhood that her adoptive parents came to the Catholic orphanage and walked up and down the aisles of cribs until little Susanna pulled herself up to a standing position, smiled at them, and reached out to them. She was nine months old, abandoned by her unwed teenage mother, and her new parents took her home.

"But I remember wondering [as a child] what would have happened if I had been cranky that day or had a load in my pants and didn't feel like smiling at strangers," she writes to us. "Would they then have chosen that smiler on down the row?"

In sometimes surprising ways, the very young adoptee's misunderstandings and confusions can continue to resonate far into the adult years. Susanna, for example, says that her adoption story still haunts her whenever she goes into a pet store and watches someone choose a puppy.

THE ADOPTIVE BOND

In their relationship to their parents, adoptees in this period of development continue to look very much like nonadoptees. Our own studies confirm this. A few years ago, our doctoral student Leslie Singer used the Strange Situation experiment (described in the previous chapter) on a group of thirteen-to-eighteen-month-old toddlers.[9] What she found was clear: the adoptees taken as a whole were essentially just as secure in their attachments to their mothers as were the nonadoptees.

One difference did emerge and achieve what social scientists call statistical significance. This occurred when Singer compared biological pairs with one subset of adoptive pairs: pairs in which the mother and the child were of different races. Even in these special cases, Singer thought the differences might have been an artifact of the experimental situation itself. To test for this, she later followed up her lab research with a more naturalistic study that looked at mother-toddler pairs in their own homes. Her hunch was confirmed. At home, she found, adoptive mothers (whether of the same race as their babies or not) were just as responsive to their toddlers, just as sensitive to their needs, just as cooperative in their styles of play, as were biological mothers.

A more recent study by another graduate student adds further support to this finding.[10] Loreen Huffman asked mothers of four-year-old intraracial and transracial adoptees to rate their children on a variety of behaviors associated with security of attachment. All the children had been placed for adoption within the first fifteen months of life, the majority within the first three months. Huffman found that a large majority of adoptive mothers viewed their children as very securely attached, whether they were of the same race or of a different race. The importance of attachment in the adjustment of young children was underscored by the finding that the mother's ratings of security and attachment was the single best predictor of behavioral and emotional adjustment among the preschool children. When children feel an emotional connection to their caregivers—whether biological, adoptive, or foster parents—they are better able to weather the stresses and strains of childhood.

The Klein family is a vivid demonstration of the way parents interact with their young children, whether they are adopted or not.

After eight years of trying desperately to conceive, the Kleins adopted Victoria, a newborn—and then Mrs. Klein promptly became pregnant. Jessica was born when Victoria was ten months old. But though Victoria often envied her younger sister for her intelligence, her looks, and her popularity, she never envied her for her status as biological daughter. This is because of the evenhanded way in which the Kleins treated both girls.

When she was twelve years old, Victoria remembered that, "Even when I was three or four, I never thought Mom and Dad treated us any different. I was Vicki and she was Jess."

SPECIAL CASES: LATER ADOPTIONS

When a child is adopted *during* the preschool years, there may be a unique set of problems in establishing a parent-child bond. This may be especially true of children born abroad, many of whom are adopted during toddlerhood or preschool years. Unlike an infant, a young child has a memory and is able to recall meaningful relationships from the past; she may grieve for months. In addition, the child was just beginning to acquire words in her native language, and suddenly finds herself in a home whose language she cannot understand.

A youngster adopted from overseas at this stage needs to mourn not only for the loss of her original family but also, in a sense, for the loss of her mother tongue—or, as one of our Korean-born patients put it, "my mother's tongue."

"Boy, did I used to give them trouble," our patient Alfonso, now ten, remembers about his first two years living with his adoptive family. Indeed, as his parents remember it, Alfonso spent the ages between about four and six having one long tantrum—a harrowing state of affairs that didn't end until Alfonso entered first grade and found an adored best friend.

Alfonso had lived with his mother, an Indian servant girl in Honduras, until he was two, when his mother lost her job and placed her son in a Catholic orphanage. He lived in the orphanage for a year and a half before he was adopted. By the time he moved to the United States, he was speaking a mixture of Spanish and Indian, neither of them very well.

When the nuns told Alfonso, then three and a half, that he was about to be adopted,

"I thought that it meant going back to my mommy as soon as I left the orphanage." Instead, he ended up in the home of an American couple he did not know. "I was nasty with them, too," Alfonso recalls. "I think I didn't want to learn English because I saw how much they wanted me to."

Newly adopted babies with memories of foster care will do better in their adoptive homes, we have found, if a few conditions exist: if the adoptive parents are sensitive and without psychological problems themselves, if the baby is healthy, and if the general environment is relatively free of discord. It's also important for agencies to provide parents with detailed information about the child's prior schedules and habits, vocabulary (what words are used to describe toileting, for instance), and the names of people who had been important to the child.

For toddlers and preschoolers, adjustment is eased if the child is given an opportunity to talk about her past in an open and nondefensive way, without having to worry that she may be betraying either her first parents or her new ones. Our patient Sheila was not given that chance. Placed in foster care at the age of two, and adopted by the foster family six years later, Sheila was never told she was adopted. Her parents believed that if she were treated as a biological child, she would never find out otherwise. But she retained vague memories of her toddlerhood that continued to confuse her until she was fifteen and discovered, by accident, that she had been adopted.

"I vaguely remembered my older [biological] brothers pushing me in a baby carriage. When I would ask my adoptive mother about this, she would say I was imagining things, that no such thing ever happened," says Sheila, now thirty-four.

And she actually remembered being brought to her new home—a memory that must have been terribly confusing to a child whose mother insisted she had had no prior life.

"I remember being put in a bed for the first time. I remember being brought to my new home. I looked at my sister [then about three] and she looked at me. She says she remembers me wearing a brown dress and brown shoes. She didn't like me. I think she was jealous. She would scratch my face all the time . . . My new mother gave me a bath and my new father carried me into the bedroom. There was a full-size bed in the bedroom and my sister and I shared it. I remember being placed on the bed and thinking there was nothing like it in the whole world. I later found out that I had lived in a shack with my biological parents, and had slept in an old dresser drawer."

To maintain the myth that Sheila was their biological child, her adoptive parents had to go through some pretty tricky maneuvering. But no matter how unlikely their explanation for confusing facts, Sheila accepted it. For instance, Sheila's adopted sister is eight months older; their mother simply told them Sheila had been born prematurely.

"I never truly believed her, I just never challenged her," Sheila says. And her last name was different from her adoptive family's. "I would ask them why my last name was different, and they would tell me it wasn't my last name, it was my middle name," she says. "I know it probably sounds kind of bizarre, but I went along with the program. My parents told me to use my biological last name and their last name on all my school papers. I guess they were preparing me for when I would be adopted and then just drop the middle name.

"One day that very thing happened. I remember my mother getting a phone call, and when she hung up she called my sister and me into the kitchen. She told us not to use our middle names anymore, just our first and last names."

At the time, Sheila was eight years old; her sister was nine.

When children are placed much later—beyond the age of two or three—these games and half-truths are even harder to get away with.

These children have memories, and may be openly grieving for the early caretakers they were attached to. Some of these children have histories, too, that make adjustment more difficult, especially if that history includes physical or sexual abuse, nutritional deficiencies, or chronic infectious disease.

Our patient Oswald was taken from his foster parents when he was two years old. The foster parents, who were white, had applied three days earlier to adopt Oswald, the son of a black "bag lady" who could not care for him. The welfare department responded to that request by removing Oswald from the white family's home and placing him with a black family that also wanted to adopt him.

The caseworkers apparently didn't think that adopting across racial lines would be in Oswald's best interest. But without impugning the good-heartedness of the black family, it seemed to us that separating Oswald from his first parents, no matter what color they were, was not in his best interest either.

When we met Oswald at the black family's home, he was huddled in a corner, completely mute, with clear mucus draining from his nose. His symptoms were a typical two-year-old's reaction to separation. Oswald was grieving for his original foster family.

EMERGENCE OF RACIAL AWARENESS

During the preschool years, children become aware of racial differences. As they look around them, they recognize that some people have light skin and others dark skin, some have straight hair and others curly hair, some have rounded eyes and others narrow eyes. And they begin to relate their own appearance to individuals around them.

"I'm like Mommy," says Karen, four. "I got long hair that's straight. I'm not like Daddy, 'cause he's got real crinkly hair."

Physical characteristics help children define themselves and make connections with others. Feelings of belonging and security are nurtured by looking like the people around you. In most families, physical resemblance among their members is taken for granted; children and parents usually have the same skin color, hair texture, eye shape, and the like. But when physical resemblances are absent, children can become confused.

Adopted children, especially those adopted across racial lines, often feel that they are different from the rest of their families because of how they look. This is most common among nonwhite children who are adopted by white parents. During the preschool years, we begin to see adopted children developing an awareness of racial differences and reacting to them.

Toni, for instance, was a four-year-old black girl who was adopted soon after birth by a white couple. Bright, outgoing, extremely attractive, Toni had been doing well until two months previously, when she began to ask questions about her appearance.

"She wanted to know if she would have white skin and straight hair when she grew up," Toni's mother said. "She wanted to know if she could have her skin painted the same color as mine."

Soon after the questions began, Toni's parents hired a black housekeeper to whom the child took an immediate dislike. Toni even kicked the housekeeper a few times, and called her "ugly" and "stupid." When the child came to our office for an evaluation, she quickly confirmed her sensitivity to racial differences. She went straight to the dollhouse we use in therapy and took away all the black dolls. "They're bad," she said. "They don't live here. Only they [the white dolls] do."

This is not to say it is necessarily a problem to adopt across racial lines; it is simply another complicating factor.

Our young patient Josie spent her first five years in rural Minnesota, where she was the only Korean child for many miles. Indeed, everyone else in her community, from her adoptive parents to her playmates, was blond-haired and blue-eyed. But when Josie was nearly five, her family moved to the East Coast, to a community with many other youngsters from Korea. The first time she played with these Korean children, her mother recalls, Josie seemed almost as though she were in shock. "Why do they look like me?" she asked. It was the first time she had ever indicated that she knew she looked different from her parents or the other Caucasians among whom she lived.

Michael, another Korean adoptee raised by white parents, also asked questions. But he was so intensely curious about what made people people that his mother was nearly driven to distraction.

"I know it's good for kids to ask questions, but I wish he would slow down a bit and give us a break sometimes," said his mother when Michael was four years old. She said his constant bombardment of questions seemed to border on obsession with people and why they look the way they do.

"How come people look different?" Michael would ask his mother. "Who makes people? Why do Korean people have different eyes? How come Daddy is bigger than you? How come you don't have a penis? Where does hair come from? How come some people's hair is black and other people's hair is not black?"

Adoptive parents may rationalize their children's questions as evidence that they fully understand the meaning of being adopted. But generally this is not true. A preschooler may recognize that Mommy is white and she is black, but this is a far cry from understanding how this difference came to be, or what it means to have another mommy who is black. As we shall see, the cognitive foundation for this type of understanding usually does not develop until the elementary school years.

Chapter 3

MIDDLE CHILDHOOD

AGES SIX TO TWELVE

My adoptive mother used to tease me all my growing-up years. She thought she was "just playing," but at five or six or eight years old, I took it very seriously. She would tell me that if I didn't behave, she'd send me back. She told me that she and my father had had a choice between me and a chimpanzee, and that they had made the wrong choice.

—Kate

The school-age child is at last becoming a citizen of the world. He now has meaningful emotional relationships with people outside the family—with friends, with teachers, with coaches. His universe no longer begins and ends with Mom and Dad. At this stage, the child is developing his own intellect, mastering skills of deducing and imagining, devising a capacity for logical thought.

Peer relationships become important, too, and the youngster wants more than anything else to conform, to be part of the group. If he's not like the other kids, he is subject to teasing—or, at the very least, to feeling "nerdy" or "weird."

Physical development plays an important role during these years. Between five and seven years of age, the brain undergoes significant maturation, which lays the foundation for the emergence of more sophisticated thinking. The muscles that control gross and fine motor coordination also mature. This allows children to master activities such as ice skating, roller skating, baseball, playing a musical instrument—all the skills that support a positive sense of self.

In addition, beginning at about the age of seven for girls and at about nine for boys, children start producing ever-increasing amounts of sex hormones. With this hormone production comes sexual development, ranging from the growth of breasts to the beginning of frequent masturbation. And sexual development is always accompanied by changes in self-image. A girl with budding breasts suddenly becomes shy about her body, and often decides that her breasts are too large, too small, too uneven, too something. A boy who has frequent unexplained feelings of aggression or sexual fantasizing also develops a new self-image—one that might include such feelings as guilt, shame, and the need for privacy.[1]

Middle childhood is often the period when being adopted is first seen as a problem. This is when the youngster begins to reflect on the meaning of being adopted—which often leads to feelings of confusion, and to feeling odd or different. And this is when the child, because of his growing capacity for logical thought, begins to realize that there's a flip side to his beloved adoption story—that in order to be "chosen," he first had to be given away.

A SENSE OF THE SELF

Between ages six and twelve, the search for self continues and becomes more refined. Two themes emerge at this point: self-concept, the cognitive awareness of himself as a unique being; and self-esteem, the extent to which he values that uniqueness. Self-concept refers to how children see themselves, self-esteem to how much they like what they see.

Self-concept is a cognitive function, and thus is closely tied to the child's maturing cognitive skills. A simple way to demonstrate a child's emerging cognitive sophistication is to ask him to describe himself. That's what John Broughtman, a psychologist at Teachers College, Columbia University, did in an experiment designed to measure how people think about themselves. He interviewed individuals from the preschool years through late adolescence and asked them questions such as "What is the self?"[2]

From the answers, Broughtman distinguished between two levels of self-awareness in school-age children. Children younger than eight offered concrete definitions that focused on gender, size, appearance, possessions, and physical activities. Five-year-old Bobby, for instance, might distinguish himself from his friend Alan because he has blond hair and a new "two-wheeler," while Alan has brown hair and an old bike with training wheels.

Children older than eight, Broughtman found, began to make distinctions between mind and body; between what they thought and what they did; between possessions and personality. Older children's self-concepts were less concrete, more self-reflective. "I can't read very well," says Josh, a ten-year-old with learning disabilities, "but the kids like me because I play baseball really good, and I joke around and make the kids laugh." Roughly between the ages of eight and twelve, children became more aware of personal characteristics in others and used them as standards for evaluating themselves.

Broughtman's study brings up a point we have observed in our own clinical work: that in some important ways, children at the beginning of the "middle childhood" period are quite different from children at the end. In terms of self-concept, physical development, interest in the opposite sex, and understanding of themselves in the context of the world around them, the age of about ten or so (slightly earlier for girls, perhaps later for boys) is an important line of demarcation. We have chosen to treat the school-age years between six and twelve in a single chapter in order to remain consistent with the Eriksonian model of child development. But we do recognize that this approach has its limitations.

Being adopted can complicate the development of self-image and self-esteem, especially when the adoptee does not look like his parents. This lack of physical similarity is a common factor in most interracial or intercountry adoptions. The racial awareness that emerged during the preschool years becomes more refined in early elementary school, and the young child might have trouble coming to terms with his self-concept. Looking in the mirror each day and seeing one set of features, and looking at other family members and seeing a different set of features, can be disconcerting, especially for the child under eight, who tends to define himself in concrete terms.

James, six, is a black child who was adopted in infancy by a white couple. For the past year, he has been preoccupied by his physical appearance. When he began kindergarten, he noticed that the other black children in the class had black parents, and that the white parents had children who were white.

"Am I black or white?" James asked his mother one day. "What makes you ask that?" she replied. "Well," said James, "black kids have black skin and black parents, but I have black skin and white parents."

James's mother reminded him that he was adopted. His birth parents were black, she said, even though she and his adoptive father were white.

"I know that," he said. "But I still don't know if I'm supposed to be black or white."

As adoptees get older and more reflective in describing themselves, they achieve a greater awareness of being adopted, and of how this unique family status is a part of their emerging self-definition.

"I know that I'm adopted; it's part of who I am," says Elizabeth, nine. "When people ask about me and want to know about me, one of the things that comes to my mind is that I'm adopted . . . Sometimes I tell them and sometimes I don't."

For some children, being adopted is a part of themselves they would just as soon forget. Conner, for example, has displayed considerable anger over the past three years. An extremely bright seven-year-old, Conner began to understand the meaning of being adopted much earlier than most children. But he has not been able to incorporate it into his self-concept in a positive way.

"I hate being adopted," Conner says. "It makes me feel different and I hate that. I just want to be like everyone else . . . I want my parents to be my real parents. Being adopted is like being punished."

For other children, however, being adopted offers a great sense of comfort; for them, adoption is security. This is especially true for children like Alicia, who at the age of ten was placed in an adoptive home after five years in foster care.

"I think about myself as being adopted now," she said right before the adoption was finalized. "That's better than thinking of yourself as being a foster child. Being adopted means 'forever,' that your parents will love you and won't send you away or hurt you, like what happened to me before . . . I'm adopted now and that makes me feel good."

SELF-ESTEEM AND THE SENSE OF MASTERY

As a sense of self develops, the evaluative component also comes into play: the sense of self-esteem. How a child feels about himself has a great deal to do with how he adjusts emotionally.

The importance of self-esteem in psychological development has been the focus of much research. In a classic study by psychologist Stanley Coopersmith, school-age boys with high self-esteem were found to be more independent, creative, assertive, socially outgoing, popular, confident, and nonconforming than boys with low self-esteem.[3] But more significantly, Coopersmith was able to derive a list of *maternal* factors that seemed to nurture a positive self-esteem in the boys he studied. Mothers of boys with high self-esteem, according to Coopersmith,

- are more accepting and affectionate toward their children;

- take an interest in their children's activities and friends;

- are generally more attentive to their children;

- set clear limits on behavior, enforcing rules in a firm and decisive manner;

- punish their children by denying privileges rather than by using physical punishment or withdrawal of affection; and

- allow their children greater individual expression, including a say in making family plans and setting their own bedtimes.

According to Erik Erikson, a child's self-concept during the school-age years develops largely through the struggle between, as he puts it, "industry" and "inferiority." For a child between six and twelve to have a healthy feeling about himself, he needs to develop a feeling of mastery—the idea that he is capable of making things that have an impact on their surroundings.

In certain cultures, "industry" might include skills such as hunting, fishing, and making clothes. For a child in North America, "industry" usually means going to school and learning to read, write, do arithmetic, and use computers. But it includes nonschool skills as well: going to Cub Scouts to learn about camping and stock-car racing; playing on a soccer team or playing Little League baseball; taking after-school classes in gymnastics, piano, or karate. The more ways in which a child, in any culture, can say, "I can do it!" or "I understand!" the more self-confidence he gains. By the same token, the more he experiences failure or finds his achievements to be downplayed or ignored, the more "inferior" he feels.

Just as school-age children attempt to gain control and mastery in school, sports, and social relationships, they also attempt to integrate into their emerging self-concepts the idea of being adopted. In an adoptive family, the struggle between industry and inferiority can be as troubling and confusing a period for the parents as it is for the child. For the first time, they may notice significant changes in their child's adjustment to adoption. As children move through elementary school, it is common for their earlier positive feelings about being adopted to give way to a sense of ambivalence.

This pattern is seen quite clearly in our patient Brian, who is nine years old. According to Brian's mother, he had always seemed happy about being adopted. During his preschool years, he would ask for his adoption story again and again, saying, "Tell me about myself." When Brian was about seven, though, his attitude changed dramatically. He no longer asked about his adoption, and the adoption storybooks—once his favorites—were suddenly hidden away. When his mother tried to talk about adoption with him, Brian quickly changed the subject.

"He seemed to have undergone a change," his mother says. "He wasn't the happy kid I knew him to be. He looked mostly sad when the issue of adoption came up, sometimes angry, too. I began to think something was wrong with him. Maybe he was having emotional problems. I also wondered if I had done something wrong. Had I pushed the issue too much or too early? Had I forced him to try to deal with it before he was ready? I was as confused and unhappy as he was."

Like many parents, Brian's mother attributed the changes in her son to either a problem in him or a problem in her. What she didn't realize, however, is that such changes are very common, and quite normal. A number of years ago, we and our colleagues Leslie Singer and Anne Braff Brodzinsky asked adoptees between the ages of six and twelve to compare the adjustment of adopted and nonadopted children.[4] Our questions were designed to measure intellectual and academic competence, popularity, emotional adjustment, self-concept, and self-esteem.[5]

Interestingly, the youngest adopted children rated adoptees as significantly better off than their nonadopted peers. In other words, they thought adoptees were brighter, happier, more popular, and more self-confident than children who were not adopted. At around the age of eight, however, this view changed. Although maintaining many positive feelings about adoption, the older children now were beginning to recognize and experience some of the more difficult and confusing aspects of being adopted—most of which were linked to a sense of loss and to feelings of being different. These include such common experiences as occasional sadness and anger, as well as increased uncertainty about oneself. The gradual shift we observed in an adoptee's attitude about adoption—which has a direct impact on his self-concept and self-esteem—occurs as part of a broader process associated with his intellectual development.

THE GROWTH OF LOGICAL THOUGHT

Middle childhood is a time of remarkable intellectual growth. Beginning at around age six, children enter what Jean Piaget called the period of *concrete operations*. This is the time when children develop conceptual skills that permit them to understand the world in a logical manner. The stage is labeled "concrete" because the child's thinking is still grounded in the things he observes, on tangible objects and events. Unlike the teenager and adult, though, the child still is unable effectively to deal with abstract principles.

The nature of this cognitive change is illustrated in an experiment made famous by Piaget and his collaborator, Barbel Inhelder.[6] They presented preschool-age children and school-age children with three empty beakers. Two were of the same height and width, and the third was taller and narrower than the other two. They filled the two identical beakers with the same amount of liquid. The children agreed that both beakers had the same amount.

As the children watched, the investigators then poured the liquid from one beaker into the narrower beaker. Of course, the liquid rose to a greater height, even though the total amount of liquid was unchanged. The children were then asked whether the two filled beakers had the same amount of liquid in them or whether one had more and the other less.

Preschool-age children, whose thought is not logical, were taken in by the perceptual qualities of the vessels. Either they focused on the height of the tall, narrow beaker and said it contained more liquid because "it goes way up here," or they focused on the short, wide beaker and said *it* contained more liquid because "it is fatter." Older children, however, immediately recognized that the two vessels still had the same amount of liquid. Because of their newly developed logical thought, they were able to understand that the two dimensions of the beaker compensated for one another—that the increase in height in the one beaker was accompanied by a decrease in its width or diameter. This awareness, known as "conservation of liquid quantity," is one of the many logical skills that emerge during this developmental period.

The growth of logical thought has a profound effect on virtually every area of a child's life. It fosters more effective problem-solving skills, increases the child's sensitivity to the perspective of others, and opens up new awareness of the self and the world in general. And for the adoptee, it helps to foster a more realistic understanding of adoption. In a series of studies with children from the preschool years through adolescence, we have examined how children come to understand the meaning of adoption and its implications for the adoption-adjustment process.[7]

Beginning at around six or seven, the adoptee can differentiate between adoption and birth as alternative ways of forming a family. In other words, he recognizes that although everyone enters the world the same way—by being born—most children become members of their family by being born into that family. He also recognizes that being adopted means having two separate sets of parents—those who conceived and gave birth to him, and those who are raising him.

Seven-year-old Emma highlights this newfound awareness about adoption.

"Adoption means coming out of your first parents and then going to live with your second parents," she says. "The first ones are the ones who made you and the other people are your parents always. They have to take care of you and everything."

Although this early distinction between birth and adoption is very important, it is only a foundation for the more in-depth, meaningful understanding of adoption that will emerge throughout the middle childhood years. From our research, we have found that between the ages of eight and eleven, the adoptee's understanding and appreciation of the implications of adoption grow at a profound rate. Along with this growth in knowledge comes a decline in positive attitudes about being adopted. Now we also begin to see the rise in psychological, behavioral, and academic problems that are more common in adoptees.

Elementary-school-age children are becoming increasingly proficient *problem solvers*. The growth of logical thought, increased sensitivity to others' viewpoints, and classroom experiences all contribute to this process. The school-age adopted child for the first time makes spontaneous efforts to seriously consider the circumstances surrounding his birth. And he thinks, also for the first time, of the unchosen options that had been available to his birth mother.

"If she didn't know how to be a mommy, then someone should have taught her," says Carla, nine. "She should have gone to school to learn—then it wouldn't have happened."

"If she didn't have enough money to be able to keep me," asks Monica, eight, "why didn't she get a job?"

"I often wonder why she and my first dad didn't get married," reflects Tim, eleven. "Together they probably would have been able to keep me. By herself it probably was impossible. That gets me angry, that my first dad probably just left and didn't care enough to try."

These simple solutions for the complex problems confronting the birth parents represent the child's efforts to understand the relinquishment and to resolve the sense of confusion and loss associated with being adopted.

A youngster's emerging *understanding of the family* also complicates his feelings about being adopted. Young children—generally those under seven—define a family primarily in terms of geography: to the child, his family comprises whoever lives in his house. Biological connection is not seen as a requirement for family membership. This means that young children easily accept their adoptive parents' assurances that they are all part of the same family and will remain so forever.

But at about seven or eight, a child begins to recognize that families usually are defined in terms of blood relationships. Seeing that they are not biologically tied to their parents, but that they do have birth parents (and possibly birth siblings) elsewhere, many adopted children begin to express some confusion about their status as family members.

"It's weird being part of something you don't know about," says Trevor, ten, who was adopted from Korea as a baby. "When we had to do a family tree in school, I didn't know what to do. I wondered whether I should have included my Korean parents. I certainly look more like them than my parents now."

In addition, this period is characterized by the development of *logical reciprocity*. Logical reciprocity underlies assumptions like the one that if Sally is taller than Susan, then Susan must be shorter than Sally —obvious to an adult, perhaps, but not so obvious to a young child. Consider four-year-old Max, the younger of two siblings, who is asked whether he has any brothers or sisters. "Yes, I have a brother," he says. But if Max is then asked, "Does your brother have a brother?" he will probably say "No." The ability to understand that the concept of brotherhood implies a reciprocal relationship—each brother must have a brother—is another example of the type of logical thought that will not emerge until middle childhood.

With regard to adoption, the development of logical reciprocity helps to sensitize the child to the issue of relinquishment. To their younger children, adoptive parents talk about the adoption by emphasizing their desire to have a child and build a family. The child, so the story goes, needed a home, and the adoptive parents chose him to become part of their new family. What usually isn't discussed is *why* the child needed a home. Once children enter into a period of logical thought, however, they realize that to have been "chosen," they first had to have come from somewhere—which meant that someone had to give them away.

During this time, children begin to understand adoption not only in terms of "family building," but also in terms of "family loss." It is this awareness that sets the stage for many of the adjustment problems seen in adopted youngsters.

Grieving for the Lost Family

As the school-age child begins to understand the logical implications of adoption, he starts to feel a sense of loss for the parents, and the family, he never knew. Even if he was adopted as an infant, even if he never met his birth mother and has no recollection of her, he still experiences—at least to some degree—a sense of loss; he still grieves.

As we saw in the previous chapters, infants and toddlers who were adopted after they formed attachments to their first caretakers do indeed exhibit grief reactions. But the idea that children adopted in the first days of life *who never knew their birth parents* are still capable of grieving for them has been difficult for many people to accept. When we first began to talk about this back in the late 1950s, even some of our professional colleagues were skeptical. How can a youngster grieve for someone he never knew? And if problems could be traced to grieving, why are they emerging seven or eight years *after* the actual loss occurred? Why didn't the child start grieving right away?

The answer is really quite simple. Unlike the later-placed child, the youngster who was placed as an infant, and who has never known his birth family, cannot grieve for his loss until he develops an internal mental representation of what it is he has lost. This can take the form of thoughts, mental images, and fantasies about his birth parents and his past. Once this internal representation develops, at around age six or seven, the basis for grieving is in place. At this point, the child is not grieving for a *known* birth parent, but for the *representation* or *fantasy* of a birth parent.

This does not mean that children who are adopted *after* infancy will also delay grieving until age six or seven. It is now well accepted that once a child begins to form an emotional attachment to a specific individual, which usually occurs as early as six to eight months of age, then separation will produce a characteristic behavioral pattern that resembles grieving: signs of protest, despair, and eventually detachment. The longer the child lives with his first "attachment figure," the greater the likelihood that he will show emotional distress if they are forced to separate. And the nature of the distress generally will be more intense, and more obvious, than that associated with loss in early adoption placement.

Curtis, for instance, was removed from his mother's care because she had neglected him, often leaving him alone when she went shopping or visiting. Although he was neglected, Curtis was quite attached to his mother, and his placement in a foster home at the age of four was quite traumatic for him. He began to wet his bed, had frequent nightmares, cried uncontrollably, and displayed considerable aggression toward the younger children in his foster family. Curtis's reactions were understandable: his relationship with his mother was sufficiently well developed and satisfying that separation from her produced a traumatic grief reaction.[8]

The grief of adoption experienced by youngsters who were placed as infants is usually, but not always, more subtle than Curtis's. Typically, adoptees placed early in the first few months of life do not express the shock, deep depression, uncontrollable crying, or intense rage that are commonly part of acute or traumatic loss associated with older-child placements. They usually show their grief through confusion, occasional sadness, social withdrawal, or periodic outbursts of frustration or anger.

The emergence of adoption-related loss during middle childhood has important implications for understanding certain trends we see in adopted children's adjustment—the sudden eruption of behavior problems in six- or seven-year-olds who previously were quite well adjusted. Parents and teachers call these kids "troublesome," "difficult," "disturbed." But when we investigate, we often find that adoptees in trouble are simply going through a period of grieving.

"I couldn't eat; I couldn't even stay in the restaurant," said Michelle, eight, who was adopted from Korea when she was six months old. "All the Orientals in there kept looking at us as if I was a freak. I looked more like them than I looked like Mom and Dad. And then I started to wonder: could they maybe even know my [birth] family?"

Michelle's tantrum in the Chinese restaurant was unlike anything she had ever experienced before. It was the first sign, in her parents' estimation, of any difficulty in her adjustment to being adopted. We consider it an early manifestation of grief.

Mental health professionals have long known that when we experience a major loss, we grieve. The stages of the grieving process have even been demarcated: first shock, then denial, protest, despair, and finally recovery or reintegration. These "five stages of grief" do not happen to everyone in precisely the same progression, nor do they always erupt with clear beginnings and clear endings. But most people in mourning do go through each of these stages in one way or another.

Still, there is great variability in the expression of adoption-related grief, even among adoptees placed as infants. For some children, there is only the slightest recognition of pain associated with adoption; for others, the pain is frequent and disturbing. And the way in which the sense of loss is dealt with is also highly variable among these youngsters. Some children are quite defensive in dealing with adoption-related loss, relying on strategies such as denial and avoidance to cope with their feelings. Others are more open and direct; they readily acknowledge the varied feelings they have about being adopted, and often seek out opportunities to talk about them.

A smaller group of adoptees are those whose sense of loss is masked by intense anger and disruptive behavior. These are the children who most often get referred to psychotherapists. They usually take on an exterior of bravado; their every gesture says, "Nothing will touch me." They are argumentative, oppositional, intensely angry, and occasionally physically threatening to the people in their lives. Although they usually deny that they have been affected much by being adopted, beneath their tough armor lies a little child who has been deeply hurt by life. Typical of such children is Evan, who at the age of eleven complains, "Even my real mom didn't want me." Children like Evan feel essentially worthless, and they cannot imagine anyone accepting them for who they are. These youngsters assume a facade of anger, defiance, and emotional distance. These are the most vulnerable children, and the most difficult to reach.

Children in our society suffer other losses, of course, such as the loss of a parent through death or divorce. But none of these other losses is quite like the loss of adoption. Our own experience tells us that from the child's point of view, adoption is by far the most complicated loss.

As described in Table 3, these three common routes of childhood loss—death, divorce, and adoption—have similarities, but they also have important differences. Adoption is at once a more pervasive loss —the infant-placed child has had no connection at all with the birth parents—and one that is more difficult to accept as permanent—since the child has a sense that restoring a relationship with the lost parents is at least a possibility. These facts, combined with the lack of any social recognition of the loss of adoption, can make this period of life very painful for the young adoptee. Often, the adoptee doesn't even know why he feels so sad or so angry; the possibility that his feelings are related to grief is too abstract for him to grasp, and he suffers his emotions without being able to put a name to them.

Table 3   The Losses of Children: A Comparison

	Universality
Divorce:	Not universal, but common
Death:	Universal, though not always death of a parent
Adoption:	Uncommon, may lead to feelings of isolation and "differentness"
	Permanence
Divorce:	At least potentially reversible, if the parents remarry; the noncustodial parent is often visited; reunion fantasies are common among children of divorce
Death:	Permanent, irreversible

Table 3 The Losses of Children: A Comparison

Adoption:	Seems potentially reversible, since the birth parents may be alive; reunion fantasies are common among adopted children

Relationship with the Lost Parent

Divorce:	A long history of a relationship before divorce affords the child a store of memories, which may help the child come to terms with the loss
Death:	A long history of a relationship before death affords the child a store of memories, which may help the child come to terms with the loss
Adoption:	No history of a relationship with the birth parents; little information about them provided by the adoptive parents; the lost parents often linger as "ghosts" in the adoptee's mental and emotional life, making it hard to come to terms with the loss

Voluntary Versus Involuntary Circumstances

Divorce:	A voluntary decision on the part of at least one parent, fostering anger toward the parents and guilt and self-blame for the child
Death:	Involuntary, no one to blame
Adoption:	A voluntary decision on the part of at least one parent, fostering anger toward the parents and guilt and self-blame for the child

Extent of the Loss

Divorce:	Partial loss of a single parent
Death:	Permanent loss of a single parent
Adoption:	Loss of both birth parents and of extended birth family; loss of cultural and genealogical heritage; sometimes loss of a sense of permanence, sense of connectedness to adoptive family, sense of self, social status

Social Recognition of Loss

Divorce:	Loss rarely recognized; few rituals or support systems exist to help the child get through the loss
Death:	Universally recognized; rituals and support systems are plentiful to help the child get through the loss

Table 3   The Losses of Children: A Comparison

Adoption: Loss rarely recognized; few rituals or support systems
             exist to help the child get through the loss

THE FAMILY ROMANCE FANTASY

For a school-age child, an especially important developmental goal is establishing himself in the world beyond the family. Between the ages of about nine and twelve, the child prepares for the move toward independence that is the hallmark of adolescence, and he does so by separating himself psychologically from the family. Peers, teachers, coaches, rock stars, and sports idols compete with parents for the child's attention. This process necessarily brings the child in conflict with his parents. He is attempting to pull away from their control at a time when his parents believe—and most people would agree—that he still needs considerable support, structure, and guidance from the family.

A common outgrowth of this parent-child conflict is the emergence of what Freud has called the "family romance fantasy." This is something that many children, adopted or not, go through. But with adopted children its resolution is more complicated, because the "fantasy" is, in large measure, real.

Biological children at about this age often have fantasies that they were secretly adopted. This usually arises after a period of conflict with their parents; it is a child's way of dealing with the unsettling fact that he can both love and hate his parents at the same time. If those nasty disciplinarians are so hateful, the child reasons, they must also be imposters; my real parents would never be so cruel.

Children often "dream of being some kind of foundling, an offspring of some family of very different social standing," wrote psychoanalyst O. Fenichel in his classic study of neurosis. "This may be either a high and especially privileged family, or a very poor and low one."[9]

The second half of the family romance fantasy is that the child's "real" parents are better than the ones he lives with. "The whole effort at replacing the real father by a superior one," Sigmund Freud wrote, "is only an expression of the child's longing for the happy, vanished days when his father seemed to him the noblest and strongest of men and his mother the dearest and loveliest of women. He is turning away from the father he knows today to the father in whom he believed in the earlier days of his childhood, and his phantasy [sic] is no more than the expression of a regret that those happy days are gone."[10]

Here's how the family romance fantasy works in a typical child raised by his biological parents. When he fights with his parents, ten-year-old Jesse is going through a necessary, though unpleasant, step on the route toward psychological independence. After the argument, he might retreat to his room and think to himself, "How could they be so mean? They don't love me. Parents are supposed to love their children; maybe these aren't my real parents. My real parents are somewhere out there, maybe royalty, maybe movie stars, certainly nicer than these two. Maybe I'm adopted or somehow they stole me from my real parents. Someday my real parents will come and rescue me and take me away from these horrible people who make me do my homework and finish my broccoli."

For a while, unable to understand ambivalence, Jesse will give all his love to those fantasy parents and direct all his anger at Mom and Dad back in the kitchen. Eventually, though, he will mature enough to tolerate ambivalence in his relationships. When this happens, his feelings about the romantic "other" parents and horrible "real" parents will start to blend together. He will gradually realize that his parents are people, sometimes lovable, sometimes not.

But when the child is adopted, it is harder to come to this resolution. There is always a mythical "other" set of parents out there who can hold on to their qualities of goodness—allowing the child to continue investing the day-to-day parents with qualities of badness.

"I keep imagining them as being important," says Gwen, eleven, about her unknown birth parents. "I used to think that maybe my father was some kind of war hero, like he went off to war and did something great, but then he died . . . and my mother was maybe a model or movie actress who was beautiful, but who worked all the time and couldn't take care of me . . . I know it isn't true, but I like to think things like that. My parents now are nice but they sometimes do things that get me really mad. They don't listen when I want to tell my side of things. They tell you to

do something and then yell if you don't do it right away. I sometimes wonder if my other parents would do that."

For many adoptees, though, the family romance is often turned on
its head. In 1977, Herbert Wieder, a New York City psychiatrist,
published several articles explaining complications in his adopted patients' fantasy lives.[11] Because they had experienced adoption as an
initial rejection by their biological parents, followed by rescue by the
adoptive parents, the children in Wieder's sample seemed to find it
too threatening to entertain feelings of anger or disappointment toward their adoptive parents. Any anger carried with it the threat of
reabandonment. So Wieder's patients reversed the traditional family
romance fantasy; for them, all the bad qualities were imagined to
belong to the birth parents.

Our own experience indicates that fantasies are not always so cut-
and-dried. The balance of good and bad qualities ascribed to the birth
parents differs from one adoptee to another, and even within the same
adoptee from one time to another. We think the predominant fantasy,
especially among adoptees who later search out their birth parents, is
simply a variation on the typical Freudian theme: birth parents who
are of humble origin though exceptionally good and caring.

A child's direction of anger depends a good deal on how he views
his relinquishment. Were his birth parents too uncaring even to try to
raise him? Were his adoptive parents too selfish to consider leaving
him where he belonged?

Children who think they were "abandoned" or "rejected" are usually angry at their birth parents.

"I hate them for what they did," says Megan, ten. "They didn't care
enough to keep me. They just gave me away, like I was ugly or
something."

"I would punch them or drown them if I could," says Drew, seven.
"They stink . . . they didn't want me and I don't care 'cause they
just stink."

Children who think they were "stolen" or "bought" are usually
angry at their adoptive parents.

"I think they [the birth parents] might miss me and maybe are looking for me," says Will, seven. "They lost me when I was little . . . The adoption people took me from them and gave me to Mommy and Daddy, 'cause they didn't have a baby. I'm mad they did that."

"It isn't fair that they could buy me just because they have more money," says Erica, nine. "Kids should be with their real parents. I'm not a toy or something you just decide to buy."

And children who think they were put up for adoption because something was wrong with *them* are usually angry at themselves.

"Maybe I cried too much or didn't eat right, or something," says Melissa, eight. "I keep thinking that I did something wrong . . . like it was my fault."

The family romance fantasy, according to Freud, should be resolved some time during adolescence. But in adopted children it can go on much longer. And, as we have seen, sometimes it plays itself out in a reversed pattern, with the bulk of positive qualities being attributed to the adoptive parents. For these children, there is usually less overt conflict in the family, although not necessarily less pain about being adopted.

THE "SEARCH" BEGINS—IN THE IMAGINATION

We are often asked, "What percent of adoptees search for their birth parents?" And our answer surprises people: "One hundred percent." In our experience, *all* adoptees engage in a search process. It may not be a literal search, but it is a meaningful search nonetheless. It begins when the child first asks, "Why did it happen?" "Who are they?" "Where are they now?" These questions may be asked out loud, or they may constitute a more private form of searching—questions that are examined only in the solitude of self-reflection. This universal search begins during the early school years, prompted by the child's growing awareness of adoption issues.

Though it is experienced by all adoptees, the mental search can at times take some rather bizarre turns. For example, seven-year-old Steven seemed to stop blinking, and his physician father was worried that Steven had developed a thyroid problem. But Steven told us that he *couldn't* blink; if he did, he said, he might lose sight of his mother passing by on the street or appearing on TV.

At this time, being adopted becomes a complex, emotionally laden issue for the adoptee. It is a time when he struggles for answers —a *search* for the reasons underlying the adoption, as well as a search for a way to integrate the fact of adoption into the child's sense of self. The process is complicated by the fact that while the adoptee is cognitively developing a new type of understanding of the world, including adoption, emotionally and psychologically he is still very much a child—and still dependent on the very people who could be most hurt by his inner explorations.

Our patient Phoebe, seven, exemplifies the conflicting emotions that many adopted children feel. Phoebe was placed with her adoptive family at the age of two and a half, so she still has memories of her birth mother, who neglected her. Her adoptive parents brought Phoebe to us because she was suffering from nightmares, separation problems, and a ravenous appetite. Notes from our very first conversation reveal how easily Phoebe swung from one extreme to the other in her thoughts about adoption.

> "I'm real happy now about being adopted," she began, "because I have a family that won't ever give me up—never. They told me."

When we asked if she ever thought about her birth mother, Phoebe thought for a moment before answering.

> "I'm kind of happy about her, too," she finally said. "Because she made me be who I am, no one else, just me. If she didn't make me, I wouldn't be me."

These responses showed Phoebe to be a thoughtful little girl with a healthy self-image. But after a while, some other emotions came to the surface. Phoebe said she was glad not to be living with her birth mother anymore because her mother moved around so much, but then she admitted that she "kind of" missed her, too.

"I would have liked to travel to Hawaii with her. She travels to Hawaii a lot."

We asked Phoebe if she had other thoughts about her birth mother. Her answer indicated an active fantasy life.

"I wonder where she is," she said. "I would like to call her up and say, 'This is your daughter, Phoebe.' She would probably say, 'Oh, I'm so glad to hear from you.' She probably would say, 'Come and visit me in Hawaii.' I wouldn't want to go because she might want to keep me, and I don't want to leave my family now. I like it here . . . but I guess I would like to see my first mom a little bit."

Children of this age feel compelled to explain their world and how it came into being. If being adopted is part of their world, they will feel compelled to explain that. For some kids, it's an intellectual exercise only, with no more emotional wallop than wondering about the stars in the sky. For some kids, it's everything.

"It's the master question of my life," said Michael, nine: "Why did she give me away?"

Some adoptive parents react to their children's questioning in ways that can turn innocent questions into major secrets. Joe Soll, fifty, the founder of the New York–based Adoption Circle, remembers asking his mother about his "real mother" when he was about seven years old.

"She got hysterical," Joe says. "That, for me, was enough, and I never asked again. I was a zombie about adoption and I turned it off, mostly." Yet he also says he remembers thinking about his birth mother, and about being adopted, "every day from the age of seven on."

Susanna, forty-four, had a similar experience. She asked about her birth mother only once, also at the age of seven:

"My mother told me that she didn't know anything about 'that woman' but that it really didn't matter because she was my mother and that was all I needed to know. That was when my fantasy life began."

Throughout her childhood, Susanna thought about who her birth mother must have been.

"I imagined that I was conceived and born in a brothel," she says, "or that my birth mother was the little old lady who lived in a shoe and had so many children [that] giving away the last one was the only thing left to do. One of my favorite fantasies was that Loretta Young was my birth mother and it would have ruined her career if she had kept me. After all, I had high cheekbones and looked good in chiffon."

THE PAIN OF BEING DIFFERENT

Middle childhood is the period when children become acutely aware of being different. Anything can qualify as "different" to a self-conscious preteen: having bangs that are too short, having freckles, wearing braces, not wearing braces. If their adoption makes them feel different, this can be a great source of stress.

Youngsters may deny feeling different because of being adopted, they may become angry about it, or they may even exaggerate it. Freddy responded by becoming the class clown. At the age of twelve, Freddy was a very funny child, yet so mature that he sometimes sounded like a boy of college age. Even his teachers and his parents said he "marched to a different drummer." Freddy told us he had cultivated his odd traits deliberately. Because his parents always introduced him as "our adopted son Freddy," he already felt different—and he wanted to wear that feeling like a badge of distinction.

Nancy, however, hated being different. Now forty-four, she still remembers being forced to convert to Judaism, her adoptive parents' religion, when she was about eight—a ritual that heightened her feelings of being outside of the clan.

"I didn't like the fact I was adopted," she says. "I felt very different from everyone else. I didn't feel wanted."

Envy and jealousy become predominant emotions at around this time. Even for nonadoptees, much of psychological growth has been ascribed to the interplay of envy and jealousy. A prominent investigator into these emotions, psychiatrist Robert E. Anderson of the Albert Einstein College of Medicine, defines envy as the painful awareness of lacking some advantage in comparison with another person, and jealousy as the feeling that an advantage the person currently has is threatened by a rival.

In our experience, envy and jealousy are inevitable in adoptees, and they emerge for the first time during middle childhood. The adoptee simply cannot be the same as the nonadoptee; this can lead to feelings of envy, diminished self-esteem, shame, and, for some, emotional paralysis and social alienation. The voices of our correspondents illustrate the pervasiveness of envy.

- "I felt different from my friends, rather 'unconnected,' envying people who had biological families."
- "I always envied other families who looked like one another."
- "I want to know all the things which nonadoptees take so infuriatingly for granted. I feel that I have somehow been robbed of something vitally important."

Schoolchildren can be merciless in their taunting and teasing of peers who are different in any way. Elementary school is when allegiances of the playground can be fiercely drawn, and anyone on the outside of the "in" group can be made to suffer. Too often, this can include children who become outcasts simply because they are adopted.

"Sometimes the kids at school tease me because I'm adopted," says Becky, eight. "When we fight they sometimes say, 'You don't even know who your mother is!' "

"Because I'm Korean and my parents aren't, everyone knows I'm adopted," says Trevor, ten. "Sometimes when I get into a fight

with someone at school, they call me 'Chink Eyes,' and make fun
of me because I'm adopted . . . I don't know what to do then."

Sometimes the taunting can be intended as good-natured, but re-
verberates in disturbing ways for adoptees. Dave, at twelve, was part
of a group of preteen boys who took to greeting each other with
curses and jeers meant to be friendly. "Hey, Dave, you old son of a
bitch!" or "Hi, you bastard!" the boys on the playground would say.
And Dave suddenly realized he didn't know whose son he really was;
he *was*, in point of fact, a bastard.

THE RESILIENT CHILD

If adoption is so stressful, then why don't all, or even most, adopted
children show serious problems? There are several reasons. First,
adoption is not usually an *acute* stressor. Most parents begin to discuss
adoption with their children during the preschool years. By the time
children are developing the cognitive sophistication to understand it,
they have lived with this rather unique status for some time. They
have grown accustomed to it, even if they have not fully compre-
hended it. As we will explain later in this chapter, children who are
placed later in childhood are more likely to experience acute adoption-related distress. So are adoptees who are not told of their adoption until much later than the norm.

Second, some home environments seem to foster effective coping
strategies in dealing with adoption. The sociologist H. David Kirk,
now retired from the University of Waterloo in Canada, has suggested
that parents who are honest in acknowledging the inherent differences in adoptive family life are more likely to create an environment
that helps to assuage the child's fear and guilt regarding his search for
answers about his origins. These Kirk calls the "acknowledgment of
differences" families, as opposed to his "rejection of differences" parents, who try to downplay adoption issues and pretend that adoptive
families are just like any other family.[12] "Acknowledgment of differences" families are, as we have seen, the families in which the child's
adjustment is easier. Families who reject differences, he says, transmit
the message—knowingly or unknowingly—that adoption must be
kept secret. Their children are more likely to experience problems in
adjustment.

Our patient Dennis grew up in a household that Kirk would have labeled an "acknowledgment of differences" family.

"When I was trying to understand why I had to be adopted," he says, "it helped that my parents, especially my mother, were always encouraging me and letting me know that I could ask them anything. I felt safe, like no matter what I thought or asked or did, like searching for my birth mother which I'm doing now, my mother would accept me."

Gwen, on the other hand, lives in an adoptive family that meets Kirk's description of "rejection of differences."

"I can't say how I really feel about being adopted to my parents," says Gwen, eleven. "They would be hurt. They make me feel ungrateful when I bring up anything about being adopted, but especially about my first mom. It's a secret in our family. That's hard, because I get upset sometimes and they don't help much with it."

Finally, there are some children who are just born "resilient." They have inherent personality traits that simply make them able to weather stressors better, including the stressor of being adopted. They are calm, reflective, able to control their behavior and emotions. These resilient children seem less affected by adoption than are more irritable, impulsive youngsters. While not denying certain negative feelings about being adopted, resilient children generally find a healthier way of integrating them into a generally positive self-image.

"There really isn't anything so special about being adopted," says Laurel, eleven. "It's just something that happened. I've thought about my birth parents from time to time, but not so much now . . . It just isn't a big deal. I know it is for some kids, but it just isn't for me."

Of course, life is not always rosy even for the resilient child. Many of the resilient children we have known go through frequent periods of sadness or anger regarding adoption issues. What makes a child resilient are his coping strategies, coupled with a fundamentally positive self-image and the availability of emotional supports.

Paul is a resilient child. From the time he was three or four, he had a remarkable ability to reflect on his own behavior, to understand his feelings and the motives for his actions. He was also quite self-confident and yet realistic in his appraisal of his abilities. As he approached age six, he began to understand that being adopted meant he once had another mother who could not care for him. According to Paul's mother, this thought sometimes made him sad—but not for long.

"I remember when I first knew about adoption—I was just about four," Paul told us when he was eight years old. "I remember thinking that my first mom put me inside my mom and that was what adoption was all about. When I was five or six, though, I knew that I came out of my first mom, but not my second mom. It was a funny feeling knowing that. I didn't know who she was. I was sad because I didn't know her, and I wanted to see what she looked like.

"Sometimes I still get sad, but it doesn't hurt too much. When my grandmother died, I was more sad, I guess because I knew her all my life. It's hard to be really sad about my first mom if I didn't know her, except when I was born.

"I don't think adoption is all that bad. Even though you don't know your first parents, you get new parents who love you, and that's what counts."

A SPECIAL CASE: LEARNING DISABILITIES

Adoptees are about four times as likely as nonadoptees to be diagnosed as learning disabled. Since the rate of learning disabilities is roughly 5 to 15 percent of the school-age population, adoptees may be at a rather high risk of running into some sort of problem in school.

Learning disability has become something of a catchall diagnosis for anyone who clearly has normal intelligence and yet is having trouble with academics. A more helpful label would relate to the specific type of learning disability a child encounters. The most common types of learning disabilities are listed in Table 4.

Table 4   Types of Learning Disabilities[13]

Dyslexia	Inability to read or spell
Dysgraphia	Difficulty translating ideas or sounds into written letters or words
Dyscalculia	Difficulty with basic arithmetic skills because of the inability mentally to manipulate numbers
Dyskinesia	Motor difficulties, poor coordination, physical awkwardness
Dysphasia	Difficulty in speaking or understanding what is said
Attention Deficit Hyperactivity Disorder (ADHD)[14]	Unusual energy and restlessness, short attention span, impulsiveness, inability to complete work

Because many of the symptoms are relatively subtle, learning disabilities may not be recognized until long after a child is in school. Indeed, it is in school that most of these problems become problems at all, grounded as they are in the successful performance of academic tasks. A child with dysgraphia would have no problems if he lived in a society in which no one wrote!

But learning disabilities seem to be associated with certain cognitive problems outside the classroom, too. Learning disabled youngsters are often plagued by poor self-esteem, have trouble making cause-and-effect connections in their daily lives, and show deficits in social judgment, peer relations, maturity, and the ability to modulate their emotions.

The causes of learning disabilities probably include both biological and psychological factors. Some learning disabilities are inherited, while others are caused by trauma to the central nervous system either during the prenatal period, during labor and delivery, or after the child is born. A third group of learning problems are associated with emotional difficulties.

Why are adoptees at increased risk for learning disabilities? For one thing, many of the personality traits that go along with learning disabilities—impulsiveness, poor judgment, immaturity—also go along with unplanned and unwanted pregnancy. Young women who give up their babies for adoption, therefore, may be more likely than other young women to be learning disabled themselves—and to pass along a genetic predisposition for this problem to their babies.[15]

Second, the nature of the pregnancy may increase the chances of an adoptee being learning disabled. An unplanned and unwanted pregnancy is inherently stressful. These young mothers are themselves often just out of childhood, and the intrauterine environment may be less than optimal for neurological development. The young mother is also likely to ignore or deny the pregnancy until rather late, which might mean she continues drinking, smoking, or eating poorly during the first or even second trimester. These prenatal factors increase the risk of central nervous system damage that might lead to some type of learning disability.

Third, emotional problems may be more likely in adoptees who become preoccupied with their adoption—and these in turn may lead to learning problems. During the elementary school years, some adoptees are flooded with thoughts and emotions about being adopted. This makes it difficult to concentrate on anything else, including schoolwork.

The presence of learning disabilities in an adopted child can have a profound influence on his adjustment. Being learning disabled may compound the child's feelings of being different. It is another form of status loss, as adoption is, and can undermine self-esteem.

"Why can't I learn like everyone else in school?" says John, nine. "It makes me feel stupid and different. I hate being different; I'm always different. First it's being adopted, and now it's this thing."

Learning disabled adoptees may also have more trouble than other adoptees in understanding adoption. They are more likely to distort information, including the facts of why they were placed for adoption in the first place. Because the "learning disabled" label already brands them, they may actually think they brought the adoption on themselves.

"I feel like I'm dumb or something, like there's something wrong with me," says Monique, ten. "I wonder whether that's the reason she gave me away . . . Maybe she didn't want a dumb kid."

When an adoptee is learning disabled and the adoptive parents aren't, trouble can erupt. The majority of adoptive parents are middle-class, with above-average levels of education. In these families, great value is placed on academic success. The presence of learning disabilities can be a serious blow to the parents' hopes and expectations for their children.

A few years ago, we saw two boys with attention deficit hyperactivity disorder (ADHD). Zachary was eight years old, and Ethan was nine. Each was a difficult child—stubborn, impulsive, fidgety, and prone to tantrums. Each was having trouble in one or more areas of school performance. Yet the ways the families dealt with their sons could not have been more different.

"When I was a child I had the same kind of problems at school, and so did my brother," said Zachary's father. "I can understand what Zachary is going through. But I'm successful and my brother's successful, and I know we can help Zachary learn to deal with this. We have to help him through this."

Zachary was not adopted, and learning disability obviously ran in the family. His own background helped Zachary's father empathize with his son's situation. His success, and his brother's, also gave him hope that Zachary would eventually overcome his handicap.

Ethan, on the other hand, was adopted. In his family, attention deficit disorder was bizarre, unexpected, alien.

"It's terrible for me to see this," said Ethan's father. "I feel disappointed having a son who may never do well in school, since academic success has always been important to me. I don't know what Ethan's life will be like; I worry that he'll never succeed at anything."

MORE SPECIAL CASES: LATE-PLACED OR
INTERNATIONAL ADOPTEES

During middle childhood, particular problems arise for youngsters who are adopted between the ages of six and twelve. Often, late-placed adoptees have had a rough time earlier in life, being shunted from one foster home to another until a family adopted them. Some have been neglected, others abused; some have been separated not only from birth parents, but from birth siblings as well. Many enter their adoptive homes with a known history of emotional, behavioral, and academic problems. All these factors can make the period of adjustment long and difficult.

Peter, for instance, was adopted at the age of six, two years after the death of his mother. His father had tried to raise Peter and his older brother on his own, but eventually realized he just couldn't manage. He gave each boy up for adoption.

At first, Peter seemed to adjust well. His adoptive parents lived in a neighborhood bursting with children his age, and their large extended families offered many cousins for Peter to play with. But about a month after Peter arrived, he seemed to withdraw.

> "He had trouble falling asleep," his mother recalled. "He didn't seem to enjoy the food. He became more and more withdrawn, even with all those children around. Even after he'd been with us for nearly a year, he still seemed like he was a stranger in our house."

When late-placed adoptees are brought from foreign countries, adjustment can be harder still. Not only have they lost the people who were important parts of their past, but they have also lost their countries, their cultures, their languages.

We first met Alfonso, a ten-year-old who was adopted from his native Honduras when he was three and a half, because he was sleepwalking. We asked him to keep a record of his dreams, and one dream was especially vivid to the boy:

> "I am in a strange city. There are twisting streets and alleys. I don't recognize any of the people. I'm half afraid and half kind of ex-

cited. It's like in a large marketplace with lots of people talking, but I can't understand them. Then I seem to hear my name, but I'm not sure. So I follow where the voice is coming from. I can't ever seem to catch up to the person who is calling me. I wake up sweating and somewhat scared."

Someone recently had said to Alfonso, "Where did you get that name?" "From my real mother," he answered, proud and angry at the same time. "Don't you want to change it to something more American?" the person asked. "No," Alfonso said abruptly.

Later, with a directness quite typical of a child of this age, Alfonso told us why he wanted to keep his name.

"How can I change it?" he asked. "What if she comes to look for me?"

Difficult as it is for parents to watch their adopted children try to deal with the pain of adoption-related loss, they can do nothing to spare them. They can, however, help ease the process by providing a supportive, nurturing environment in which the emotional storms of grieving can be weathered. When parents ask us what they can do to make this period easier for their adopted children, we tell them to be available to their children, listen to them, help them clarify their emotions, and accept whatever feelings they are expressing. By their nonjudgmental responses, parents can show their children that these ups and downs are normal, real, acceptable—and temporary.

Chapter 4

ADOLESCENCE

AGES THIRTEEN TO NINETEEN

In my adolescence, I never felt "good enough." This was the irony of being labeled "special." I felt I could never live up to the label. I lived under a tyranny: "If I just do it better, I'll be loved."

Because I felt less than whole, I sought friends or boyfriends to fill in the missing pieces of my self-esteem, to make me feel good about myself. I sought approval and craved affection in my relationships. However, since only I can ultimately accept and like myself, this seeking approval from others failed to help me feel better in the long run, and made the relationships very difficult.

—Kate

Huge changes occur in the years between thirteen and nineteen. The adolescent growth spurt—which in many children begins years before the actual "teenage" years—accounts for a faster growth rate than at any time since the prenatal period. The hormonal surges of puberty change a child's contours, textures, and fantasies. The new ability to understand abstract concepts leads to a preoccupation with values, morality, and the self. And the heightened importance of the peer group makes teenagers intensely social beings.

ARE TEENAGERS IN TURMOIL?

Because of all these changes, the popular image of adolescence is as a period of great personal and family turmoil. The physical and emotional changes of puberty, in this view, make a teenager feel totally out of control. And in her agony and confusion, she lashes out at the people she knows best—her parents.

Conventional wisdom has it that during the teen years mood swings, including outbursts against the family, are typical. Eda LeShan, whose advice column has appeared for years in *Woman's Day* magazine, is one of the many experts who say teenage years are hell for a family. In her own household, she has said, she and her daughter never exchanged a civil word with one another while the girl was between the ages of thirteen and fifteen.[1]

But in the psychological community, there is a good deal of controversy about just how inevitable—or even how common—adolescent turmoil really is. Although psychoanalytic theorists like Erik Erikson and Anna Freud made much of the "crisis" of adolescence, many empirical psychologists have failed to find convincing evidence of prevalent psychological upheaval during the teenage years.

In our own clinical and personal experience, we have found that while emotional turmoil is unquestionably a reality for some teenagers, it is far from universal. The way young people react to the changes of this age—physical, psychological, and social—can be highly individualistic.

Careful research confirms this clinical impression. Daniel Offer of the University of Chicago, for example, interviewed seventy-three teenagers for his classic study of normal adolescence.[2] The majority of them, he found, worked through the issues important to them—issues of identity, relations with parents, peer interactions—with few outbursts or rebellion. Changes during these years tended to be gradual and undramatic.

UNIVERSAL CHANGES OF ADOLESCENCE

The physical changes of adolescence, in contrast, are indeed dramatic and universal. Teenagers grow at a rate comparable to their growth rate during the first six months of life. For girls, the "adolescent growth spurt" begins between the ages of nine and eleven, peaks at an average age of twelve and a half, and is generally completed between fifteen and eighteen. Boys start shooting up between about eleven and fourteen, peak at about fifteen, and have usually finished growing by the age of twenty or twenty-one.

Not only are teenagers' bodies lengthening, but they're changing shape and proportion. Girls grow curvier, boys more muscular. With the onset of puberty, secondary sex characteristics develop. And new hormonal surges often have behavioral effects as well: a greater interest in finding a sexual partner, an increase in sexual fantasies, and the beginnings of sexual experimentation. Increased muscle mass may also create anxieties in the children when they "lock horns" with their parents, as teenagers often do; their sheer physical power in relation to their once all-powerful parents may truly startle them.

At about the age of twelve or thirteen, a new phase of cognitive development also begins. Jean Piaget called this style of thinking "formal operations." As opposed to the "concrete operations" typical in younger children, "formal operations" are highly abstract. Abstract thinking allows a teenager to focus on matters of morality, philosophy, and esoteric questions such as "What is the meaning of life?"

Youngsters of this age are inclined to make more abstract moral judgments than they had at earlier ages. For younger children, "right and wrong" are defined in terms of behavior that does or does not get punished. In early adolescence, "right" is whatever behavior wins approval or is in keeping with the social order. But by late adolescence, youngsters begin to define right and wrong independent of group or social values. This is known as "postconventional morality," involving a personal abstract set of principles such as justice, equality, and honor.

The code of ethics that becomes so important during adolescence explains, at least in part, why peace and democracy movements throughout the world have traditionally been led by students. At no other age are people as willing to sacrifice themselves for a higher good than during adolescence.

Psychiatrist Eugene Pumpian-Mindlin calls adolescence a period of "omnipotentiality"—a time when anything seems possible. As he puts it, the youth is convinced "that he can do anything in the world, solve any problem in the world if given the opportunity, and if it is not given he will create it. There is no occupation which is inaccessible, no task which is too much for him. Nothing is impossible."[3]

Interestingly, the values that teenagers embrace typically resemble the values with which they were raised. Though the popular image of the "generation gap" conveys a tendency for teenagers to reject all their parents' values as shallow and materialistic, research has shown that most teenagers actually accept the same values as their parents.

Issues of identity also come to the fore, including not only questions like "Who am I?" but "Who am I in relationship to other people?" This carries with it an exploration of the youngster's racial or ethnic identity. She wonders what it means to be black or Jewish or Hispanic or Irish, and how she can make that identity meaningful in her daily life. These explorations can become quite complicated for a teenager who is adopted, especially if she was raised in an interracial family.

Most teenagers also strive toward establishing independence and autonomy. They begin to pull away from the control of authority in general, and parents in particular. Once again, this developmental task is complicated for an adopted teenager, since so many of the crucial decisions in her life—whether she should be placed for adoption, which family should adopt her, whether she should have access to information about her birth parents—have been under someone else's control.

Peer relationships become extremely important now. Teenagers start confiding in friends rather than simply "playing" with them, as they did in earlier childhood. Their one-on-one relationships become more intimate, while at the same time "cliques" and "crowds" begin to take on a new significance. During adolescence, it's important to feel in step, to have no characteristics that will set you apart from your peers. This desperate need to conform can also present special problems for an adopted teenager, who may feel different from other people because she doesn't know much about her past. And if she lives in a community where few other youngsters are adopted, then being adopted is just one more way in which she can feel "weird."

"It feels funny being different, not like everyone else," says Jason, who is thirteen. "It's not like you're some star athlete or a rock star or something—that's the good kind of being different. When you're adopted, it's like someone didn't want you."

This is not to say that adolescence, for adoptees or nonadoptees, is merely one interminable struggle. While some adults may remember their teens as the worst years of their lives, others remember them as the best: the time of limitless possibility, endless introspection, intense friendships.

How Do I Look?

The teenage years are when kids can stand at the mirror for hours looking at a cowlick or a pimple. Every gesture they make, teenagers think, is being watched; the egocentricity of this age is astounding. If each of these kids is being watched, have they ever wondered who is out there in the audience?

As they spend hours primping and fretting before the mirror, adolescents tend to rely on physical markings as keys to their identity. But during this stage, many of these familiar landmarks shift right before their eyes. The adolescent growth spurt can add six to eight inches to a teenager's height in the space of one eruptive year; the hormonal changes of puberty can radically alter a young girl's or boy's silhouette, skin texture, hair. Coupled with a teenager's intense need to conform, or at least to be accepted by her peers, the sudden physical changes of adolescence can be disorienting indeed.

When an adopted child grows and changes in adolescence, and begins to spend more and more time thinking about her looks, she may be troubled by the fact that she doesn't seem to fit in physically with the rest of the family. This is what happened with Elliot, fifteen, who was always bothered by people's comments that he looked just like his father—comments he always felt were untrue.

People tell Elliot "you look so much like your dad" so often that it makes him uncomfortable. He knows that to the extent they do resemble each other, it is simply a matter of blind chance. Indeed, the frequent comments about his resemblance have made him feel *more* different from the rest of his family rather than less so. If he were really a full-fledged member of the family, why would so many people feel compelled to point out the apparent similarity?

Elliot was always on the tall side, and his adoptive family tends to be short. The older he gets, the more he grows. And the more he grows, the more out of place he feels in his own family. His height makes him feel as though he literally "sticks out like a sore thumb." As he grows, innocent comments about his resemblance to his father seem to him more and more forced and less and less true.

Many adopted teenagers react quite differently from Elliot to the fact that they resemble family members. Russ, for example, always took great comfort in the fact that in hair color, body size, and physical features, he looked as though he had been born into his adoptive family. But when he was seventeen, he made a comment to us that made it clear that he still felt like an outsider, no matter how things appeared.

"It's important to look like your parents," Russ said. "Most people take it for granted, they never even think about it. But I've had to think about it."

Russ was acutely aware that fitting into his family was something he could not take for granted.

Elana had the opposite situation—she looked quite different from her parents. When we first met Elana, at fifteen, we were struck at once by her beauty. Elana had a doll's face, fair and freckled, with thick red hair and sapphire-blue eyes. Compared to her parents, who were dark-haired and olive-skinned, she inevitably stood out. Elana always had trouble feeling a part of this Sephardic Jewish family. Her celestial beauty was frequently remarked upon by total strangers. From the time she was small, people would approach the family and say things like, "How can these be your parents? You don't look a thing like them!"

Elana's parents adored her, and her grandmother made no secret of the fact that Elana was her favorite. But the bizarre backhanded compliments that friends and relatives bestowed on her seemed to draw a wedge between Elana and the rest of the world. People would say to Elana's mother—who had had five miscarriages before adopting Elana—things like, "How lucky you are not to have gone through all the stress of pregnancy and the pain of delivery. Here you have this magnificently beautiful child without doing any of the hard work!"

The vast difference between her looks and her parents' led Elana to believe that she did not belong to their orderly, intellectual, honorable world.

"I don't have to listen to you! You're not my real parents!" she would shout when she broke a household rule. "I'm just a kid; I just want to have a good time."

Elana considered the world divided into "workers" and "players." Her parents were workers, and she believed her birth mother—and therefore herself—were players.

She knew her birth mother was a hairdresser who had conceived Elana after a one-night stand. With this scanty information, Elana concocted an entire story: her mother, she reasoned, was a fun-loving type who didn't pay any attention to rules or academics. Her mother was the exact opposite of everyone in Elana's adoptive family.

Victoria, fifteen, also wants to find her birth mother in order to make a physical connection. But she is more interested in a connection to her physical self in the future than in the here and now.

> "I'd like to see my birth mother," she says, "so I'll know what I'll look like when I get older."

Victoria's younger sister Jessica is their parents' biological child, and she looks exactly like the girls' mother. This accentuates Victoria's feelings of looking unlike anyone else in the family.

> "Jessica can tell what she's going to look like by looking at old pictures of Mom," Victoria says. "I would like to have that kind of feeling, too."

Because teenagers are so focused on their looks, adolescence can be an especially troubling time for the transracial adoptee. For dark-skinned children raised by light-skinned parents, or Oriental children raised by Caucasian parents, the obvious physical differences that set them apart from the rest of the family can cause confusion.

> "When we walk down the street, everyone knows I'm adopted," says Josh, a fourteen-year-old Korean boy who was raised in a white family.

Not only are transracial adoptees physically different, they are culturally different, too. And because adolescence is the period when cultural, ethnic, or racial identity comes to the fore, the conflict between the child's ethnicity and the family's can be another source of trouble. Issues of identity can get confused for youngsters who look one way and are raised another.

The family that raised Josh, for example, was Jewish, and when Josh was thirteen his parents wanted him to be bar mitzvahed. But the process was an agony for the boy, who was the only Oriental face in the entire congregation.

> "I'm not even really Jewish," he told his parents. "It's like a lie for me to be up there reciting from the Torah."

Not every transracial adoption leads to such conflict, though. The healthiest adjustments are made among children whose families have managed to redefine the very meaning of family. When people adopt children across racial or cultural lines, they no longer are just a white or a black family. They become a multiracial, multicultural, multiethnic family. The differences among family members should be celebrated as an inherent part of the human condition, and the culture from which the adopted child originates must be brought into the family in meaningful ways, through holiday celebrations, trips to the country of origin, and frequent interactions with other children of similar background.

But a transracial adoptee's adjustment cannot be determined solely by how well the parents incorporate the child's background into family life. Indeed, we know of many cases where even within the same family, two adopted siblings in exactly the same situation resolve their search for a racial identity in quite different ways.

In the Hartman family, for instance, both Stevie and John were born in Brazil and adopted at birth by white parents. But a family vacation to Brazil when the boys were fifteen and thirteen, respectively, made Stevie anxious and withdrawn while it gave John a sense of his cultural history that he found reassuring. The difference could probably be traced to the boys' different personalities rather than to anything their parents said or did.

The Whittier family was in a similar situation. Mr. and Mrs. Whittier were affluent white professionals who adopted two mixed-race children in infancy. Both of their children were born to white mothers and black fathers; both of them, by the time they were teenagers, clearly looked black. But the older child, Daniel, had problems resolving his racial identity crisis, while his sister Samantha had no trouble feeling herself to be black, even though her parents were white.

> "I look black, but I can't even dance," complains Daniel, who is now eighteen. "I'm not interested in rap music; I don't like to hang

out." Daniel has accepted his parents' mainstream, middle-class values, and he says the blacks in school consider him "an Oreo—black on the outside, white on the inside."

But although Daniel's interests and values are more white than black, he has not been totally accepted by the white kids at school either, especially since he has started to date. The white girls he asks out seem friendly and interested, but Daniel gets the clear sense that their parents would be unhappy about their daughters dating him. Recently, he has compromised by dating Asian girls and befriending Asian boys. "They're the other oddballs at school," he explains.

Samantha, who is sixteen, has grown up in the same family as Daniel, lived in the same community, and gone to the same school, yet she has no confusion about her racial identity. She associates primarily with black kids, and Daniel envies her clear sense of herself as a black female.

"It's easy for Samantha to fit in, but not for me," Daniel says. "She has plenty of people to hang out with, but not me. She feels black; I don't."

Clearly, racial identity within a transracial adoptive family is handled in different ways by different individuals—even within the very same family. Not everything about an adopted teenager's adjustment can be traced to things within her parents' control.

RESOLVING THE IDENTITY CRISIS

The term "identity crisis" was made famous by the psychoanalyst Erik Erikson, who described it as the time during adolescence when kids begin to wonder, "Who am I?" This question means not only "Who am I now?" but also "Who will I become?"

The notion of identity is not as simple as Erikson's popularizers would have us believe. Most of us don't achieve a uniform Identity with a capital *I*, but instead come to think of ourselves as different "I's" in different contexts. We might have an occupational identity, a sexual identity, a religious identity, an identity having to do with interpersonal commitments or basic values or other aspects of our lives.

To achieve an identity, an individual must integrate these various aspects of the self with each other over different points in time. For the adoptee, there's another element, too. The self as a family member is an important component of identity, but the adoptee has two families: the one she knows and the one she doesn't know. To ask "Who am I really?" is to ask a question to which there is often no good answer, because the adoptee has been cut off from the people and information that can help provide such an answer.

The "identity crisis" that begins in adolescence can be resolved in one of four ways, according to psychologists such as James Marcia of Simon Fraser University.[4] The ideal is for the individual to confront the issue of who she is, explore alternatives, and commit herself to a particular set of values. The confrontation, though, may be incomplete, the exploration of alternatives halfhearted, or the commitment delayed or unsuccessful. These different ways of coping with the identity crisis essentially fall into four categories:

1. IDENTITY ACHIEVEMENT. This occurs when an individual consciously experiences a crisis and tries to resolve it by exploring alternative roles. The identity achiever asks herself, "What do I believe in?" and then tries on different values and ideologies. After experimenting, she is ready to make a commitment to a particular identity and a particular set of values. This usually doesn't occur until after adolescence; most people who will experience identity achievement do so beginning in the college years.

2. MORATORIUM. The individual in moratorium also confronts questions such as "What do I believe in?" But for various reasons, she has yet to achieve any resolution or to commit herself to a particular path. Being in moratorium is not a long-term solution, since to remain in crisis is inherently destabilizing and uncomfortable. Eventually, the person in moratorium will move on to either identity diffusion (explained below) or, more successfully, identity achievement.

3. IDENTITY FORECLOSURE. This individual looks as though she has achieved a solid identity, since she has made a commitment to a set of values, a career path, or a role in life. But this commitment occurs prematurely, before the person has had a chance to experiment with alternatives. An actual "identity crisis" was never recognized or confronted; the individual has taken on an identity the way she would

buy an off-the-rack suit of clothes. The classic example of identity foreclosure is the young person who goes into the family business not because she's thought about it but because it's always been assumed that she would.

4. IDENTITY DIFFUSION.   This person not only avoids confronting an identity crisis or seeking out alternatives (as happens in identity foreclosure), but is unable to make a commitment to a particular identity such as a career, a sexual orientation, or a set of moral values. She finds nothing inherently attractive enough to be worthy of even her temporary attention. Identity diffusion comes about because a youngster lacks either a support system that would allow her to ask troubling questions or a parent figure sufficiently appealing to identify with. The child moves through adolescence unsure of what she wants, unwilling to confront the options, unable to identify with a nurturing figure because none is available.

Identity achievement can occur at different stages in different aspects of identity formation. An individual might have achieved a moral identity, for instance, while remaining in moratorium regarding an occupational identity and in diffusion regarding a sexual identity. This is a dynamic process that continually evolves—from evaluation to resolution, from disruption to reevaluation—throughout adolescence and into adulthood.

Adopted youngsters are no different from others in their patterns of identity formation. But when adopted teenagers ask themselves "Who am I?" they are really asking a two-part question. They must discover not only who they are, but who they are in relation to adoption.

Among adoptees, identity achievers tend to be those whose families allow them to discuss adoption and help them come to a resolution about how being adopted does or doesn't fit into an overall sense of themselves.

Our patient Russ, now twenty-two and about to graduate from college, has asked questions about his origins from the time he was in elementary school. His parents, an accountant and a secretary, always answered his questions openly, going so far as to accompany Russ to the town where he was born and to visit the hospital of his birth. During late adolescence, Russ went into therapy to try to get some understanding of what being adopted meant to him.

"It's strange," he said recently, "but after all my years of questioning, I'm not really interested in searching anymore. I guess I'm satisfied now that I pretty much understand what being adopted means to me."

The fact that Russ is an identity achiever, though, does not mean he is a static or rigid young man. For the time being, he has achieved a relatively stable resolution to his questions about being adopted. But his healthy curiosity continues, and will probably erupt again at some time in the future. Maybe later, he says, after he has established himself in a career and a family, he will actively try to seek out his birth parents.

Many other adopted youngsters, especially those we see in our practices, experience a continuing sense of uncertainty about what it means to be adopted. Typically, this happens either because their parents have not been sufficiently open with them, or—more often—because the information they need to resolve some of their questions is not readily available. These young people continue to search, either in thought or in actions, for their origins. They are in a state of moratorium.

Kristin, a seventeen-year-old who was adopted as an infant, is typical of a teenager in moratorium. She has always had an active, and contradictory, fantasy life about her birth family. She dates it to when she was eleven and the butt of much unpleasant teasing from her classmates about not knowing who her "real parents" were.

"I spend a lot of time thinking about all the possibilities, about what happened, what she was like, why she made her decision," Kristin says.

In Kristin's imagination, sometimes her birth mother is extraordinarily wealthy and wonderful, and her adoptive parents are keeping her from the life of luxury that is her due. Sometimes, though, she has quite the opposite fantasy: her birth mother is a slut, a worthless promiscuous woman, and her adoptive parents have rescued Kristin from a depraved and deprived existence.

Kristin is not that unusual, even regarding the extremes to which her fantasies take her. She represents an adolescent in identity moratorium.

"The most difficult thing about being adopted is that there's no real information," she says. "I have scraps here and there, but nothing that seems real to me. I often feel empty inside."

Like many youngsters in moratorium, Kristin is confronting her troublesome issue directly. She has joined a teen support group, talks to her parents about what it means to be adopted, has solicited more information from the adoption agency. And even though she has not yet pulled everything together in a way that she finds meaningful, she continues to search for answers.

"I've got to understand it," Kristin says. "Otherwise how can I really know who I am?"

On the other hand, Gregory, nineteen, is another adopted youngster in moratorium whose situation is quite different from Kristin's. Gregory, who is black, was adopted by a black family at the age of seven. In the previous two years he had lived with two foster families; before that he lived with his biological parents, a mother who was a drug addict and a father who physically abused him.

"Being adopted, it's not the same as if you were born into the family," Gregory says. "You just don't feel as though you actually belong here. The more you think about it, the more confusing it gets. I keep searching for a reason that will help me to understand why it's all happened. I can't find it. It's very frustrating. I'm sort of angry about it a lot. Sometimes that's when I get into trouble."

Like many adolescents in moratorium, Gregory keeps searching for answers to the question of why—why he was abused, why he was relinquished, why he was sent to live with this new and still-unfamiliar family.

Another significant group of adopted teenagers are in a pattern of identity foreclosure. When asked, these youngsters often deny that adoption means much to them. "Do you think about being adopted much?" a friend might ask, or, "Do you wonder about your birth mother?" "No, not really," they might say. But on further questioning, these youngsters often turn out to have accepted their parents' attitudes toward adoption rather than investigating adoption issues on their own. They tend to live in families where there's been relatively little discussion about adoption, which carries the underlying message that this is not a polite topic of conversation. Many of these adolescents feel that to be too curious about adoption is to betray their parents, or would disrupt a family harmony they feel is somewhat tenuous. So they don't bring up the subject, and if they think about it they feel guilty. They experience a strong sense of identity as a member of the family, and prematurely commit to an identity that has precluded any sense of what it means to be adopted.

Many youngsters in identity foreclosure make reasonably good adjustments throughout the teenage years. But often, as we will see in subsequent chapters, the landmarks of independent adulthood—marriage, parenthood, the death of the adoptive parents—shake the very foundation of their personal meaning.

Joe Soll, the adoptee advocate we met in the previous chapter, seemed to be a psychologically well-adjusted teenager even though he was in identity foreclosure. His problems with his sense of self emerged in a physical, almost metaphoric way: he simply stopped growing. At the beginning of high school, Joe was just four foot six and weighed only seventy pounds. His parents took him to a university medical center to consult with an endocrinologist.

> "The specialist told them that I had all the growth potential necessary and that it seemed that I was worrying about something," Joe recalls. "I knew what I was worrying about . . . [I was] spending a lot of energy denying and repressing my adoption pains."

When Joe finally left for college, where he was free of his parents' influence, he blossomed—literally as well as figuratively. During his years in college, Joe grew fourteen inches.[5]

Adoptees take on an identity prematurely in response to subtle— and sometimes not so subtle—pressure from their families to accept their point of view without asking any questions. These youngsters tend to be fearful of exploration, or to feel guilty about their curiosity.[6]

"There is nothing I could do about it; it's over and done with," says Frankie, sixteen, about his adoption. "I would just open up a can of worms. I have a good life, my parents have given me a good life. Why should I run the risk of screwing it up by letting myself think about the past?"

For Frankie, thinking about the past is a frightening prospect. Much better, in his opinion, to focus on the good life he lives now rather than the life he might have lived or the reasons for his relinquishment.

Identity diffusion among adoptees is, along with moratorium, probably the most typical pattern we see in our clinical practice, because a youngster in this state so clearly is a youngster in trouble. The identity diffuse individual seems to be floundering, with no clear path for herself. She is unrealistic about where she has been and where she is going, and lacks a clear sense of what she believes in or who she is.

Robert, for instance, was a good student through elementary school but began growing increasingly uncomfortable about his place in the family beginning at about the age of fourteen. Like many other teenagers, Robert began to question his parents' values. They were too materialistic, he believed, too concerned with what others thought. Like many other teenagers, Robert began to reject their rules and curfews. But unlike many other teenagers, he also began to wonder whether he belonged in such a "shallow" family at all. After all, he reasoned, he was adopted as an infant; this wasn't his "real" family.

"I just want to be on my own," he says. Now eighteen, Robert has dropped out of college during his first semester, and has rejected everything important to his adoptive family. Yet he has no interest in finding his biological family either. He says he wants to be a musician, but he bases that goal on eight months' worth of guitar lessons. He is unable to form a plan, unable to consider what his options are, unable to say what he believes in other than that it's not what his parents believe in. When alternative paths are suggested to him, Robert grows anxious; when he's asked to make a commitment to something, he cannot. Robert is in a classically diffuse identity state.

During the teenage identity crisis, being adopted can take on an added pain: a sense of having lost not only your birth parents but also a part of yourself. Adoption experts have called it "genealogical bewilderment," this feeling of being cut off from your heritage, your religious background, your culture, your race. If adopted children are—or feel—different from their families in any of these group identities, this genealogical bewilderment can become nearly overwhelming.

Kimberly was raised in an affluent home, but at the age of thirteen she started running away from home to stay with friends on the wrong side of the tracks. She shunned the bright, accomplished girls she had befriended earlier in her childhood, and instead hung around with kids on the verge of flunking out of junior high.

"I feel more comfortable with people like them," she told her mother. "I think they're more like me."

Kimberly's "bewilderment" came from her uncertainty about just where her unique set of talents, abilities, and perspectives came from. Am I like my birth family or my adoptive family? she wondered. The characteristics of her adoptive family were seen and experienced daily; the traits of her birth parents were wholly unknown. That is why Kimberly felt so confused.

Although adolescents have begun to achieve Piaget's cognitive stage of formal operations, the questions raised by the bewildered adoptee are so basic that many regress to a more concrete cognitive style when trying to confront them. Issues become black and white; it seems to adoptees that their "good" side must come from one family, the "bad" side from the other, and the only question is which side is the "real" them. Knowing how literal and specific many adoptees in this situation can be, even sophisticated teenagers, we asked Kimberly's mother to tell us Kimberly's adoption story.

"Your mother was not married when she had you," went the story Kimberly had been hearing since the age of five. "She was too poor to take care of you." If her mother was poor, Kimberly reasoned, then she must be poor, too. When she was sixteen, she changed economic classes entirely; she married a high school dropout from a blue-collar family.

The Family Romance Fantasy Continues

As we saw in the previous chapter, most children have resolved the "family romance fantasy" by the age of ten to twelve. By the time they enter adolescence, they have come to accept that their parents can have two sides: they can be both nurturers and disciplinarians, both good guys and bad guys.

For adoptees, though, the family romance fantasy often isn't resolved until some time in adolescence. Indeed, it often goes on well into adulthood. This is because the existence of an actual second set of parents, the birth parents, makes the family romance fantasy much more difficult to resolve. As the adolescent struggles to break free of her adoptive family's rules and restrictions, the adoptive parents become easy targets—and the birth parents become more and more idealized.

When this happens, it becomes more and more difficult to unite the two conflicting sets of emotions the child feels about her parents. Her family romance fantasy is not really fantasy; she does in fact have two different and possibly quite opposite sets of parents. Unable to accept her ambivalent feelings toward the people she loves and depends on, the adopted adolescent continues to maintain a split view of her family—and, by extension, of herself.

"I just don't relate to my parents and they don't understand me," says Denise, fourteen, one of three adopted children. "I think sometimes they enjoy hurting me; they seem to go out of their way to do it."

Denise is a troubled, angry, oppositional child, but she blames most of her problems on her adoptive parents. Her birth parents, she says, are another matter entirely; she imagines they would understand her.

"The blood relationship would make a difference. They could just be with me and they would know what I needed, not like my adoptive parents."

In Denise's view of her life, her adoptive parents are the villains and her biological parents the potential saviors.

With maturity and the accumulation of life experiences, adolescents eventually come to understand that ambivalence is common and acceptable. At this point, they may accept the fact that they sometimes hate the very parents they love. But until they get to this point —as most of them eventually do—life with a teenager can be an emotional roller-coaster ride.

SEXUAL EXPRESSION AND THE "BAD SEED"

Sex can be a loaded topic for any teenager, but especially for one who's adopted. Adopted teenagers who were born to teenage mothers may feel the cycle repeating itself in their own sexual behavior. Adoptive mothers who agonized over their own infertility may feel jealous and resentful of their daughters' developing fecundity. Adoptive fathers who feel stirrings of attraction for their daughters may be confused when the incest taboo that ordinarily quells such feelings has no real relevance. An adoptee's emerging sexuality can be a complication for the whole family.

Some adoptive parents may watch their teenagers for signs of sexual experimentation as proof that the "bad seed" planted by their teenage birth parents has finally borne fruit. This is especially likely if the adoptive parents know their child is the product of promiscuity, rape, or incest.

Selma, who is now fifty-seven, remembers her mother's perplexing behavior when Selma was in ninth grade. Now, in retrospect, she realizes that it was in a way her mother's fear of Selma's "bad seed" coming back to haunt them all.

Selma and her classmates were preparing for a hayride. She had asked Bobby Henderson, a new cute boy in school, if he would go on the hayride with her, and he had said yes.

"I was so excited," Selma recalls, still bubbling at the memory. "All the other girls were envious of me."

But Selma's mother told her she could not go on the class hayride. "Only bad girls go to hayrides," her mother said—a totally confusing statement, since the entire class was going on this school-sponsored event. "You'll have to call this boy and tell him you can't go."

Nearly forty years later, Selma finally understood why her mother had been so angry about that innocent first crush. When her adoptive parents died, Selma wrote away for her birth certificate. Her birth father's last name, it turned out, was Henderson—the same last name as the boy she had wanted to take on that hayride.

A teenage patient of ours, Sally, was a victim of her own feeling that she harbored a "bad seed"—and a famous one at that. When she was sixteen, she began having sex with some of the boys in her crowd, and behaved seductively with everyone—her teachers, her kid brother, her psychiatrist.

Sally's parents were worried about the kids she hung around with, who liked to drink and take drugs, and about her poor grades. In addition, the child was making life miserable for her family. She verbally and sometimes physically pushed around her frail, rather meek mother, and she was merciless in her taunting of her thirteen-year-old brother, who was also adopted and was no match for her intellectually.

After a few visits, we discovered that much of Sally's behavior could be traced to her especially intense fantasy that her birth mother was Marilyn Monroe. This conviction went back to junior high school, when Sally chose Marilyn Monroe as the subject of a class project. Since then, she had been collecting Marilyn books and memorabilia, and began to dress and behave as she assumed Marilyn had.

But Sally was an intelligent girl, and she knew this was impossible; she was born in 1974, twelve years after Marilyn Monroe died. In her more reasonable moments, she chose to believe that her birth mother simply *looked* like Marilyn Monroe, as Sally believed she herself did, and was still living quietly in Delaware waiting to be found.

Other forms of sexual behavior that can be traced to adoption can be even more troubling. Some teenagers defy the incest taboo because they are not biologically related to their adoptive family. Some deliberately become pregnant to undo what they feel to be their birth mother's mistakes. And some go in the opposite direction, shying away even from healthy sexual experimentation because they are so aware of where that landed their birth mothers.

- When John was nineteen, he announced that he wanted to marry his sixteen-year-old sister. "We're both adopted, so we're not really brother and sister," he reasoned.

- When Jill was fifteen, she deliberately became pregnant. That was the same age her birth mother was when she had Jill. "I want to do for my baby what my birth mother wouldn't do for me," she explained.

- "I was a virgin when I got married," recalls Susanna, now forty-four and the divorced mother of two teenage boys. "There was no way in hell that I was going to be faced with the possibility of having to give a child up for adoption. I was also going to prove to my mother that I was no slut like my birth mother was supposed to have been."

When Kelli, an adopted adolescent, got pregnant by accident during her senior year in college, she wanted to do what she considered the "right thing"—to bring the baby to term and put it up for adoption. But she disappointed herself by failing to have "the courage my biological mother showed, and to make someone else happy too." Kelli was afraid to tell her parents, who were devout Catholics, about her unplanned pregnancy, so she had an abortion and kept it a secret.

"I ended up marrying the father a couple years later," says Kelli, now twenty-six and the mother of a two-year-old with another on the way. "I think if I had had the baby, we would have ended up keeping it together. I will always feel an empty space in our family."

If the adoptee entered the adoptive family in middle or late childhood after a history of physical or sexual abuse, the fear of the "bad seed" may be especially profound. For both the parents and the adolescent, these fears reemerge during adolescence when the child starts developing sexually.

Hannah, sixteen, was placed at eight as a foster child with the family that subsequently adopted her. She had a history of sexual abuse by her biological mother that began when Hannah was six and continued during her visits home until she was eleven. Hannah since has had a succession of emotional problems—she became sexually active at twelve, ran away from home on several occasions, and made three halfhearted suicide attempts. But one recent episode troubled her as no earlier ones had. After a fight with her current boyfriend, Hannah slept with two boys in one night to get back at him. "I am my mother's daughter," Hannah says, verbalizing for the first time her dread that like her mother, she is becoming sexually out of control.

First Signs of an Active Search for Birth Parents

Kit, at the age of sixteen, started running away from home. With her extraordinarily red hair, she believed that by running away, she would increase her odds of bumping into her birth mother—a woman Kit thought would be easy to spot because she, too, would have bright red hair.

Though it is not the norm, some adoptees start an active search for their birth parents during adolescence. Indeed, sometimes a teenager's newly emerging disruptive behavior can really be a search in disguise.

Every teenager we have worked with we have helped to search, at least in the sense of clarifying his or her feelings about being adopted. Psychological searching is an inherent part of clinical work with adoptees. In a few select instances, we have gone a step further—actually encouraging teenagers to begin an active search for their birth parents. We have done so, of course, only when we thought it would resolve their problems dealing with issues of adoption, and only in collaboration with the child's adoptive parents.

Finding their birth parents—either discovering more information about them or actually making direct contact—can be an enormous relief for a teenager. A search can help simplify the adolescent's task of separating from the family. It gives the teenager something to separate *from*. Without knowing who the biological parents are, the adopted teenager sometimes gets the frustrating sense of pushing against a vacuum.

This activated "search" can take many forms. So can the definition of a "successful" search. It doesn't have to result in direct contact with the birth parents. Even if relatively little information is available, the family can still visit or learn more about the places that are part of the child's history.

Pamela, fifteen, had many of the questions other adopted teen-agers have: What did my mother look like? Why did she give me away? Where did I come from and what was it like there? Who were the people who talked to my mother? We felt that Pamela needed more information about her birth, and her parents agreed. But adoption records in Minnesota, as in most states, are sealed, and the adoption agency that placed Pamela wasn't willing to open them. The staff was, however, willing to talk to her.

Pamela and her parents made the trip to Minneapolis, where Pamela was born, on a holiday weekend. The family visited the hospital where she was born, walked through the neighborhood around the hospital, and stopped in at the adoption agency. Two counselors who were with the agency fifteen years earlier still worked there; though they didn't work with Pamela's birth mother directly, they did remember her, and Pamela took their pictures.

"I know more about my history now," Pamela says, even though most of her questions remain unanswered. "At least when I say I was born in Minneapolis, I have an idea of what the city is like."

Sometimes it's impossible to get any of the information needed to mount an active search—the adoption agency or private intermediary won't cooperate, the parents have no leads, essentially there's nothing but a blank wall. But we have found that even an imaginary activated search gives teenagers permission to think about their birth families and to work through their feelings about being adopted. We some-times help initiate such imaginary searches by having our patients write letters.

The letters involve a two-way correspondence between the adoptee and the birth mother. *The adoptee writes all the letters*—that is, the letters to her birth mother and the birth mother's letters in response. The entire correspondence reflects the adoptee's feelings and fanta-sies. Sometimes, some meaningful changes in her attitudes toward adoption come out in the course of the letter writing.

When we asked Lori, sixteen, to write letters to her birth mother, we observed over the course of nine months that Lori gradually came to accept the fact of being adopted and the uncertainties about her past. The information Lori started out with was scanty: she knew her birth mother had been nineteen, her birth father had been in the military, and that she had been born in a small Southern town.

Lori, the older of two adopted girls, first came to us because she was rude, defiant, depressed, and failing in school. She had low self-esteem and sometimes thought of suicide. Shortly after her first visit, we asked Lori to write to her birth mother:

> Dear I-don't-know-what-to-call-you,
>
> It's really strange writing this letter. I don't know you and you don't know me, but I am part of you and you are part of me. I have so many questions to ask. Why did you give me up? I guess it must have been for a good reason. I think about seeing you, but I'm afraid you won't want to see me.
>
> I think about you all the time, like what you look like and what you like to do. I like to cook and wear weird clothes. Do you?
>
> I don't feel like I'm like anyone here. I mean my adoptive parents. I guess they're okay, but they're not like me. I can't relate to them. I miss you and want to see you. Please write to me.
>
> Love, Lori___?___
> Your daughter

A week or two later, Lori composed the following imagined response from her birth mother.

> Dear Lori,
>
> What a wonderful surprise!!! After all of these years, and now I've found you, or at least I have heard from you. I am so glad you wrote. I think about you, too. I think about what you are like and what life would have been like if you had lived with me.
>
> I want to see you too. Please write back soon. I love you.
>
> ??
> Your mother

Two months into therapy, Lori's parents acknowledged for the first time that they had seen the birth mother's name written in the margin of one of the papers the adoption agency had forwarded. They had never told Lori this before. For a while, Lori used her birth mother's last name as her own. Then she composed this exchange of letters.

Dear Mom,

I can't believe it. I know your name now. My adoptive parents never told me that they knew your name. They hid it from me. I wonder what else they know that they haven't told me. I can't trust them. I have a name now, my own name. I feel like it's me, like I know about who I am, at least part of who I am.

I'm glad you thought of me all these years. It makes me feel like you wanted me. I still don't understand what happened, though. I get confused when I think about it. You must have had a good reason not to care for your own daughter. I guess you were too young or something. Tell me about yourself in your next letter, okay?

I love you,
Lori

She responded to herself in a surprising way—telling *herself* how important it was to be patient with her adoptive parents, even though they angered her by withholding information about her birth mother's name.

Dear Lori,

I am so glad you found out who I am. That makes me more real to you. Don't be too angry at your parents, your adoptive parents. They probably thought it was best to hide my name from you, like maybe you would come and look for me or something.

I was too young to take care of you. I was only a teenager myself. I wasn't married and no one could help me. I didn't want to do it, but everyone said it would be the best thing for you. Please understand.

Maybe you could come and visit me soon. What do you think?

Love,
Mom

Seven months later, just prior to termination of therapy, Lori wrote to her birth mother, addressing her not as the intimate "Mom" but by her first name—the way you would address a peer.

Dear Claire,

It's been a while since I wrote to you. Many things have changed. I'm planning to look for you soon. My parents have agreed to help me. They have called the doctor in North Carolina who delivered me. He said he might help us. I guess I may never know the answer to my question—why it happened. Maybe there isn't an answer.

I'm still confused, I still can't stand my father. He makes me sick sometimes. But I like my mother now. Don't be mad at me; she will never be my real mother. You always will be, I know that. But I can talk to her, and that helps.

Things are better at school. My grades are okay. I can't wait to finish, though. I really don't like school. I don't like the rules, and the people telling you to do this and to do that. But I can stand it for another year.

Don't be surprised if you get a call from me soon. Well, maybe not too soon. It may take a while to find you. I just hope we can. I only hope you want to see me. But even if you don't, I will be able to handle it. At least I'll know where you are and that you really exist.

Love,
Lori

These letters are important signposts of Lori's progress in therapy. Over the course of nine months, she shows increasing tolerance—for her parents, for the fact that she may never find her birth mother, for the unanswered questions that still loom. She is no longer using her birth mother's last name, but has incorporated it as her middle name. She has come to accept herself as a part of her adoptive family, and yet feels connected (through her new middle name) to a partially known past.

MOVING TOWARD ADULTHOOD

As an adolescent matures and develops interests and abilities distinct from her family's, she may start feeling a new curiosity about her origins. If this is who I am, she might wonder, what was there in my unknown past to make me this way? A need to answer this kind of question is what usually drives an activated search during late adolescence.

During college, for instance, Sharon became interested in art and art history. The more she painted, the more she wondered where this talent came from. Sharon's adoptive parents were both practical, solid, wholly inartistic people. So what made Sharon so interested in painting and drawing? To answer this question, Sharon mounted a search, which ended five years later with the painful discovery that her birth mother had died in a car crash at the age of thirty-eight.

It turned out, however, that Sharon's birth mother had begun painting at exactly the same age Sharon did. Her mother's father was an amateur painter of enough local note that he was commissioned to paint murals in two churches in her hometown. Finding this out gave Sharon permission to round out her identity as an artistic individual. In addition, when Sharon met the members of her birth mother's extended family, nearly sixty in all, her new relatives all acted as though they were seeing her mother's ghost. Sharon resembled her mother not only physically but in her every gesture, in her smile, in her facial expressions, in the sound of her laughter.[7]

Sometimes the new interests of adolescence work the other way. Instead of catapulting the teenager to search, these interests can so preoccupy an adolescent that adoption takes on less importance rather than more.

"I'm getting less curious every year," says Quintana, sixteen, in *How It Feels to Be Adopted*. "One reason might be because I don't really have much time to do a lot of detective work. I was more interested when I was 11 or 12."[8]

Quintana, the daughter of authors Joan Didion and John Gregory Dunne, still does allow herself fantasies of a reunion with her birth mother, though. If she found her "real mother," she says, "I would put one arm around Mom and one arm around my other Mommy, and I'd say, 'Hello, Mommies.' "

Part II

THE ADOPTED
ADULT

Chapter 5

YOUNG ADULTHOOD

THE TWENTIES AND THIRTIES

With the death of my adoptive father last November, when I was twenty-seven, I found I needed to feel that I belonged to a community. Now, in young adulthood, it matters to me that I don't look like someone—if not my adoptive mother, then someone in my family, an aunt, a cousin.

I have a lead on where my birth mother might be and how to meet her. One of the most important things to me in this would be to be able to look at someone's face and see my own features reflected. To see a real, physical, tangible connection in this way has become quite important. Of course, intellectually I know that even if I do find her, we may not look that much alike. Yet emotionally I fantasize about such a connection.

—Kate

As young people move into adulthood, the separation from their parents is—ideally—successfully accomplished. They can set forth into the world as truly independent people, beginning careers, establishing homes, creating new bonds.

Changes happen rapidly now. A young adult evolves into a member of a couple, a person with a career, eventually, maybe, a parent. Each of these changes can rock any prior sense of stability or inviolability as the young adult struggles with a changing definition of himself.

A young adult becomes an increasingly abstract thinker, one who sees inherent contradictions in people and ideas and seeks to resolve those contradictions. This "dialectical" approach to thinking often helps the young adult accomplish some of the primary psychological tasks typical of this age span. These tasks include the broadening and consolidation of a sense of identity, not only at a particular point in time but also as part of a meaningful transition from the individual's past to the future.

People of this age tend to see themselves largely in relation to other people. This is true of both men and women, but especially true of women. The intimate relationships of young adulthood lead, for most people, to marriage. Young adults also may take on new self-definitions as the nurturers of others by moving into parenthood or some other caretaking role. They also become members of the larger community, taking on responsibilities of civic activism and social commitment. Friendships become deeper and more meaningful, as do careers—two more aspects of the consolidating sense of self.

A stage-by-stage description of the developmental tasks of young and middle adulthood, put forth by Roger Gould in a book called *Transformations*, presents the twenties and thirties as decades of great turmoil.[1] According to Gould, people between twenty-two and twenty-eight develop their independence by making commitments to their careers and their families; between ages twenty-nine and thirty-four, they question all those commitments. The early thirties, Gould says, is a period of reconsideration, when people typically have second thoughts about their marriages, their jobs, their roles in life. Such thinking can result in great soul-searching and a reexamination of earlier choices.

There is still more turmoil in the late thirties, when a person becomes urgently aware of being closer to the end of life than to its beginning. During this period, roughly between ages thirty-five and forty-three, people might make new choices—getting divorced, going back to school, quitting their jobs to start their own businesses—that will take them down totally new paths from the ones they started off on in their twenties.

For the adoptee living through these tumultuous decades, life changes may in turn reactivate adoption issues the individual had thought were long ago resolved and forgotten. Little empirical data exists about how adult adoptees handle the developmental tasks of the twenties and thirties, which is why we solicited comments from adult volunteers for this book. Prior to this, most studies done were limited to two rather restricted populations: adult adoptees who had searched for their birth parents (and had joined support groups to do so, making it easy for the researchers to find them) and adult adoptees in psychotherapy (who were also rather easy to find). As this chapter will show, the volunteers who have helped us in researching this book —who in general are neither in therapy nor members of support groups—nonetheless invoke many of the same issues and concerns expressed by these earlier research subjects.

When Are You a "Grown-Up"?

The variation even in the legal definition of what it means to be "adult" indicates how unsure we are as a society of just when someone qualifies as fully mature. The various rights and responsibilities of adulthood are conferred at many different ages: typically, you can drive a car at sixteen or seventeen, but you can't vote or join the military until you're eighteen, and you can't drink alcohol or draw from your trust fund until you're twenty-one. Even chronological age, then, is no guarantee of being treated like an adult in all spheres of life.

Perceived age is another matter entirely. Some twenty-year-olds are still in school and totally dependent on their parents for support, while others are already employed, married, possibly even parents themselves. And some thirty- or thirty-five-year-olds, victims of a condition that has been popularized as "the Peter Pan Syndrome,"[2] insist that they "still feel like a kid" and cannot take on the responsibilities that are part of being truly grown up.

In the past generation, a new transitional period between adolescence and young adulthood seems to have emerged, especially among the middle class. That period is known among developmental psychologists, such as Kenneth Keniston, as the period of "youth."[3] A young person in this stage is no longer a teenager, but is still not ready to take on mature responsibilities like a job, a home, a marriage, and a family. "Youth" exists primarily as a by-product of protracted schooling; a full-time student, of whatever age, usually isn't ready for the various demands of independent adulthood.

The developmental tasks of "youth" are introspective, while during early adulthood a person's concerns are mostly logistical—how to pay the mortgage, how to raise the kids, how to get a promotion. In this sense, "youth" is something of a luxury; only if you're not struggling to support yourself are you granted these years to "find yourself."

Robert J. Havighurst, a psychologist at the University of Chicago, has listed the tasks that differentiate "youth" from "early adulthood."[4] From his list (Table 5), you can see how hard it is to anticipate someone's psychological stage of development based on age alone.

Imagine two quite different twenty-three-year-old women, and you can see the point. Karen has a husband, a house, a baby, and a part-time job as a beautician. Meredith is going to medical school, living at home, being supported by her parents, and unsure whether she will ever settle down and start a family of her own. Both women are twenty-three, but their inner lives are no doubt worlds apart. Developmentally, Karen is a young adult, and Meredith is still a "youth."

Table 5   Youth Versus Young Adulthood: Different Developmental Tasks

---

The Tasks of Youth
>   Learning to take responsibility for yourself
>   Establishing an identity
>   Developing emotional stability
>   Getting started on a career
>   Establishing intimacy
>   Finding a mate
>   Maintaining your own residence
>   Establishing ties to a social community
>   Deciding on parenthood

The Tasks of Young Adulthood
>   Selecting a mate
>   Learning to live with a marriage partner
>   Starting a family
>   Rearing children
>   Managing a home
>   Getting started on an occupation
>   Taking on civic responsibility
>   Establishing a social network of friends

Generally speaking, "youth" is a developmental phase of the middle class. Blue-collar workers who start working right after high school graduation can't afford it. The notion of "youth" is still so new that developmental psychologists haven't come up with a way to incorporate it into the traditional view of adult psychology. Bear in mind, as we describe the developmental tasks of the young adult, that for some protected individuals these tasks don't really become paramount until the late twenties and early thirties.

A DIALECTICAL THINKING STYLE

Among the cognitive changes that characterize the twenties and thirties is a growing sophistication in thinking style. Until recently, psychologists believed that cognitive development ended with the consolidation, soon after adolescence, of Piaget's "formal operational thinking"—the ability to reason hypothetically and abstractly. Indeed, the abstract skills developed during adolescence do become elaborated during young adulthood.

But now many developmental theorists believe that adults engage in a form of thinking that is qualitatively different from formal operational thought. Several psychologists, such as the late Klaus Riegel of the University of Michigan and Dierdre Kramer of Rutgers University, have proposed a fifth stage of cognitive development: the stage of dialectical thought.[5]

The emphasis on dialectical thought runs counter to Piaget's emphasis on equilibrium as the optimum state for the mature thinker. Riegel proposes, instead, that the mature mind seeks stimulation, which comes about from the recognition of intellectual conflict. We are by our nature problem-solvers, according to Riegel, and we seek out contradiction as the foodstuff that fosters the growth of intellect.

Dialectical thinkers not only can see the dynamic tension of apparent contradictions; they actually relish that tension. It is only by seeing and embracing opposites that the mature thinker can discover new ways of making sense of the world and of the self. Conflicts are inherent in daily life, emerging as a result of the incongruities that are part of issues in morality, ethics, politics, religion. The equilibrium celebrated in Piaget's formulation is static and dull, according to this line of thinking; it is only through creative tension that new ideas can emerge.

Dialectical thinking may be especially helpful for the adult who is adopted. The adoptee lives with incongruities.

- He has an amended birth certificate that says he was born to his adoptive parents, yet he knows he was born to a different set of parents.

- He was told as part of his adoption story that he was relinquished because his birth mother loved him, yet he knows that when *he* loves someone he wants to be near that person, not far away.

- He was told how much his adoptive parents wanted him, yet he knows that the other side of his adoption story is that his birth mother apparently did not want him.

These incongruities are often difficult for the school-age child or adolescent to accept. But the mature adult, who has developed a dialectical approach, is more likely to find a way to resolve these apparent paradoxes.

The form of resolution depends largely on the adoptee's personality. Some adoptees may simply accept the ambivalence inherent in being adopted. Others, who remain unsettled by disequilibrium, use the conflicted emotions as motivation to search for their birth parents.

THE SEARCH FOR IDENTITY CONTINUES

For most young adults, the Eriksonian struggle for identity, begun during the adolescent years, continues. The focus now is different, however. While the adolescent "identity crisis" involves primarily a definition of the self—with the teenager asking such questions as "Who am I?" and "Why am I here?"—the mature identity crisis focuses more on the self *in relationship to others* and in the context of a broader society. There is also a greater emphasis on integrating the various "selves" an individual represents—the self in career, the self in relationships, the self in terms of a set of moral values. And there is more emphasis on establishing a continuity of self over time—today's "self" in the context of who you were and who you will become.

For the adoptee, there is another task of integration as well. The adult adoptee must incorporate his identity as an adoptee into his broader sense of self, so that the notion of being adopted takes its rightful place in his life. Sometimes the adoptee has so little background information that the question "Who am I?" seems all but unanswerable.

Jamie, for instance, ran into a blank wall when she requested birth information from the adoption agency that placed her.

"I feel like a cereal box with no ingredients," says Jamie, who is twenty-four. "Even my furniture has a tag that says what it's made of. And written on the tag is, 'Do not remove.'"[6]

In an attempt to consolidate his identity, the adult adoptee tries to use his past as a springboard to understand his own future. If he has no information about his past, he begins to feel physically cut off from a part of himself. That is why so many young adult adoptees use corporeal phrases to describe their identity discontinuity. Our patients and research subjects tend to describe their feelings in this way:

- "Part of me is missing."

- "There's a hole inside me."

- "I feel that something's been cut off."

- "It's like an amputation."

For many adoptees, the loss of part of themselves is felt intensely, almost physically, as they become self-reflective adults.

This is how Lynn put it, commenting on the way she felt when she was twenty-seven and sought out some new information about her birth parents.

"To say that having this information was important to me is an understatement. It seemed to fill some kind of empty space in me that I didn't even know existed. It was like I had been walking around with holes or parts of me missing without actually realizing it. Suddenly someone hands you a piece and you realize it's part of you and it fits one of the holes. Amazing!!"

SEEKING AND ACHIEVING INTIMACY

During this time of life, the young adult strives to establish intimate relationships, both sexual and nonsexual, with other adults. According to Erik Erikson, an intimate relationship is characterized by warmth, mutuality of feeling, and deep commitment. Earlier in life, an individual forms intimate attachments with parents, siblings, peers, and, during adolescence, sexual partners. In adulthood, these relationships deepen and new attachments develop, to spouse, to children, and to a career. These become the bonds of adulthood, through which most people find meaning in their lives.

Intimacy seems to emerge differently for men and for women. For most men, intimacy is achieved only after the adolescent identity crisis is resolved, because for men true intimacy usually implies the integration of an established identity with that of a loved one. But women are different. According to psychologist Carol Gilligan of Harvard University, most women develop a sense of identity and a capacity for intimacy at more or less the same time.[7] This happens because women usually consider identity to be tied closely to intimacy; they define themselves largely by their ability to establish and maintain close, lasting relationships.

Intimate relationships are different from the romantic attachments of the teenage years. True intimacy involves mutuality, a concern for the beloved person as much as for oneself. And true intimacy means touching the deepest, hidden parts of each other. Many times, entering into an intimate relationship will force someone to admit secrets he has kept hidden even from himself. For an adoptee in a new intimate relationship, this can mean expressing feelings about being adopted that had previously been dormant or suppressed.

For a relationship to be truly mutual, both parties must reveal aspects of themselves. Adoptees, then, must at least tell their partners that they are adopted—an admission that sometimes causes great pain, as happened in the case of Beatrice.

"When I first married," Beatrice says, "I was afraid to tell my husband that I was adopted."

Even though her husband accepted the fact of her adoption, she perceived another problem. She dreaded having some previously unknown genetic defect suddenly emerge in her own children.

"I was afraid to start a family," Beatrice says. "How could I explain a child that didn't look like me? Consequently, I have never borne a child. I regret that."

True intimacy requires a strong sense of identity. And to the extent that identity is compromised for adoptees—or, for that matter, for any adult—the ability to find intimacy is compromised as well. This problem helped account for the attachment patterns of Catherine, a twenty-two-year-old woman who was unable to hold on to any intimate relationship for longer than a few months.

Catherine's pattern with men had been repeated again and again since adolescence. She would fall head over heels in love with a man, get intensely involved for months at a time, and then become dissatisfied as suddenly and as completely as she had fallen in love. What set off her dissatisfaction was the suggestion that her partner was willing to make an emotional commitment. She would panic.

Adopted as an infant, Catherine never trusted her partner's ability to live up to his promise to be there for her. Commitment was a concept difficult for her to understand. Because her birth mother couldn't commit to her, Catherine doubted whether anyone could—and doubted whether she herself was even worthy of commitment. So whenever a relationship reached a "serious stage," she would pull back emotionally.

"I want to leave them before they leave me," she explains. "That way, I'm the one in control."

The prospect of intimacy can create an inner crisis for some adoptees. The adoptee has accumulated many losses over a lifetime—the loss of his birth family, the loss of a personal history, the loss of status, the loss of stability within his adoptive family, the loss of self. Because he has already lost the first intimate relationship, the one with his birth mother, he may hesitate to embark on another. If that first relationship ended in grief and pain, who is to say the next one will be any different? This estranged feeling may continue even in adoptees whose adoptive parents embody the very meaning of commitment. Despite his adoptive parents' steadfast support, he may still, at some irrational and inarticulate level, feel abandoned.

Rosie, a twenty-three-year-old newspaper reporter, believes her fierce independence comes from the isolation she feels as an adoptee. Within her own family, she was especially isolated, because her older and younger sisters are both her parents' biological daughters. While she has always had some close friends, Rosie says she is ultimately a loner.

> "I eat alone, vacation alone, take walks by myself, see movies alone—all activities my more extroverted friends would never attempt by themselves," she says. "I only share my feelings with those I am extremely close to (parents, best friends, long-term boyfriends)—and on anonymous surveys."

Her independence sets her apart from her sisters, who like to talk about whatever is on their minds. She now shares an apartment with one sister, and the difference in their intimacy styles has led to some strain.

> "She wants to 'share' constantly," says Rosie. "While she is comfortable detailing each day—its various ups and downs—I close myself off. Not only do I fail to give an account of my own feelings, but I can barely tolerate her constant outpourings."

Intimacy requires an ability to trust, to take the chance that your partner will not reject you or your feelings and ideas. But even in the closest of relationships, differences and misunderstandings do occur, and tempers may flare. Usually, these normal ruptures are minor and temporary, and healing occurs swiftly. But for some people, even the threat of a rejection brings forth old memories of prior rejections, and small tiffs turn into major problems. For adoptees who spend their lives feeling, on some level, rejected by their first intimate contact, this tendency can make subsequent intimacy difficult to achieve.

PARENTHOOD: UNDOING PAST MISTAKES

If there's one thing that makes a young person truly cross the threshold into adulthood, it's becoming a parent. Until the moment of a child's birth, it's easy for some young people to remain carefree and somewhat frivolous far longer than they should. "I feel like a kid myself; how could I be a grown-up?" these twenty-five-year-olds declare. But after a child is born, there's no turning back. The reality of a baby's total dependence forces a redefinition of the self as a more mature, responsible adult.

But while parenthood offers an unprecedented chance to look toward the future, it also offers many people a chance to look again at their own past. By the bearing and raising of children, people in a sense renurture themselves. Parenting provides an opportunity to revisit old issues in a new context, perhaps to undo the mistakes that had been made by their own parents as they make decisions about how they will raise their children.

When the new parent is an adoptee, this universal urge to undo his parents' mistakes means not just the mistakes of the adoptive parents, but those of the birth parents as well. Sometimes this desire is expressed quite literally.

Beth, twenty-three, got pregnant out of wedlock. When she considered her options—marrying her boyfriend, having an abortion, keeping the child, placing the child for adoption—the latter choice was rejected out of hand. The thought of relinquishing her child brought back her own sense of loss. Beth said she didn't want to repeat the choices that her birth mother made. So she chose to have an abortion.

"I'd rather abort my baby than have it go through what I experienced," she said.

In contrast, Miriam, who also got pregnant out of wedlock when she was twenty-three, chose a different way to avoid her birth mother's "mistake"—she opted to keep the child. This meant she had to move back into her parents' home, quit her job as a legal secretary, and work at a night job while her mother could watch her baby.

Interestingly, Miriam has responded to her pains and struggles not by feeling superior to her birth mother—who didn't go through these hardships to be able to keep Miriam—but by feeling a new empathy.

"My real mother probably didn't have the choices that I had," says Miriam. "It's not such a stigma to be a single mother, the way it was twenty-three years ago. I'm sometimes still angry at her for giving me up. But I also feel more sympathy for her now, and more love. I would like to hug her and tell her that I understand."

For the adoptee, becoming a parent raises some issues that are different from the ones raised for new parents who were not adopted. Even while planning a pregnancy, and certainly as the due date approaches, an adoptee may think for the first time about the possibility of passing on genetic problems he knows nothing about. The absence of a genetic history takes on a greater magnitude when it is cast in the context of the next generation.

"It's one thing to be a second-class citizen oneself," says Betsy. "It's quite another to condemn one's children to no information or heritage."

Once an adoptee has children, the void in his own past is no longer his alone—it becomes his children's legacy.

"Without a past, I wondered about the future," recalls Nancy about her first pregnancy. "As a pregnant mother I worried about what hereditary surprises would occur. I resented not knowing even what color eyes the child would have."

Pregnancy may be the first time an adopted woman confronts the lack of knowledge about her own genetic background.

"Naturally I was concerned with my first pregnancy," says Ruth, who had four children in eight years. "When the doctor asked for background, I said, 'I don't know. I was adopted.' He said, 'You don't know anything?' I said, 'No.' He said, 'We'll play it by ear.' He just made very light of it."

The birth of a child often brings the adoptee into contact with the first person to whom he is biologically connected. This can have a profound effect. Adoptees know intellectually that they are not biologically related to their adoptive families, but many never allow themselves really to examine what this means to them. The birth of a child may force an adoptee to confront for the first time the lack of a genetic bond to the people who loved and raised him.

"You can't imagine what it was like when my daughter was born," says Lynn, now forty-three. "I realized that she was part of me, flesh and blood. She carried my genes—both good ones and bad ones—and would begin to resemble part of me, both physically and behaviorally, as she started to grow. When I realized this, I was surprised by my sense of jealousy."

Lynn stunned herself by resenting the security her baby would know that came with living with her biological parents.

"All my life I had lived at a disadvantage," she says. "I never knew who my biological parents were, what they looked like, what they did, what skills and talents they possessed, what shortcomings they had, etc. The funny thing is that I never consciously focused on these issues when I was growing up."

Soon after her baby was born, when she was twenty-seven, Lynn began a search for her birth parents.

Unlike Lynn, other adoptees focus on the issue of genetic isolation when they are growing up. And they think, after a good deal of internal turmoil, that they have come to some satisfactory resolution. The birth of a child, however, may reawaken the issue all over again —in a way that is just as startling, and just as painful, as if it were being confronted for the very first time.

"I had terrible postpartum depression, worse than any of the 'moods' I had gone through in adolescence," Maria recalls. "I think it was because I was grieving all over again for the fact that I didn't have what my baby had—a mother who wanted him and kept him."

Adoptees who are new parents tend to focus on the biological connection to their child, especially on the physical resemblance. They may make much of the fact that there is a resemblance, and make much of the fact that there is not a resemblance. Gerri, for instance, was devastated when her firstborn did not resemble her. She had been hoping that motherhood would give her her first taste of a real physical, biological connection to another person.

"When people said my daughter resembled my husband more than me, it made me feel very isolated," says Gerri, twenty-seven. "It was as though I were not even human."

Becoming a parent is often one of the landmarks of adulthood that pushes an adult adoptee to search for his birth parents. He searches to discover the genetic legacy that is being passed on to his own child, or to develop a connection to the past as he moves ahead into the future, or to try to undo the mistakes made by the birth parent who gave the adoptee away. When this happens, parenthood for the adopted adult can stir up a maelstrom of confusing emotions.

These feelings don't always erupt when the first child is born; sometimes they take a few years to percolate. Melanie, for instance, had two boys at home—ages two and four—when her third child was born. But this one was a daughter, and she brought to the fore all of Melanie's uncertainties about her own birth.

"I felt the overwhelming need to know more about myself," says Melanie, twenty-nine at the time.

Not only did she now realize how hard it must be for a mother to part with a baby girl, but she wanted a legacy to pass on to her daughter.

"I felt that somewhere there was a woman wondering where her child was and if she was okay."

Becoming a parent almost always makes the adoptee reconsider his relationship not only with his birth parents, but also with his adoptive parents. Even if the adoptee has had a healthy and supportive relationship with his parents, becoming a parent of a *biological* child may make him question the security of the adoptive bond.

"After having my own child, I really wonder about the differences between biological and adoptive mother-child bonds," says Kelli, twenty-six. "I've spent a lot of time with children, and 'loved' some of them, but never the way I love my little boy. It means a lot to me that he is my only *blood* relation I know."

How is it possible, Kelli wonders, for a mother to adore a child so completely if there isn't a blood bond between them? How could her adoptive mother have loved her as much as Kelli loves her own son?

PURSUING A CAREER IDENTITY

Early adulthood is a time when people choose a job path and develop a career. For some adults, the answer to the question "Who am I?" is determined largely by what they do for a living. So the choice of a career, at least for these people, is closely linked to the search for an identity.

A young person's career plans are often shaped by the influence of family life—watching parents and older siblings at work, talking to relatives, trying to match the parents' hopes and expectations with the young person's own talents, desires, and goals. Often, the adult child's choices fit in quite nicely with the parents' dreams for the child. But sometimes the fit is poor.

A "poor fit" between the parents' vicarious ambitions and the young person's own plans can be resolved in one of several ways. Sometimes the conflict is openly acknowledged and—depending on the young person's personality and the family's style—is resolved either through discussion and compromise or through outright rebellion. Sometimes the conflict is repressed. When parents are so controlling that they brook no discussion of the issue, and when children are so eager to please that they don't even acknowledge a different goal for themselves, the young adult takes on a career identity in the "foreclosure" pattern described in the last chapter. For a while, it looks as though everyone is happy. But eventually, problems almost inevitably erupt.

In adoptive families, our own experience suggests, a "poor fit" between parents' and children's goals may be more likely than in nonadoptive families. Following happily in your parents' footsteps might be more difficult if you don't share your parents' genes, since many basic skills, talents, and even interests have been shown to have at least a partial biological basis.[8] If an adoptee is forced to pursue a career because his parents insist on it, it will be difficult for him to integrate his work identity with other conflicting aspects of his identity. If he sees himself as down-to-earth and a voice of the people, for instance, he may have trouble reconciling that with a career in corporate law.

This is what happened, at least temporarily, to Gary, a young man we met when he was twenty-four. Gary's adoptive parents were professionals—his father was a successful attorney, his mother a nutritionist—who saw a college education as their son's passport to the future.

Gary was never a good student. He hadn't been diagnosed as learning disabled, but he had academic difficulties that probably stemmed from a mild learning disorder. Whatever the explanation, Gary struggled through high school, and after his freshman year in college he dropped out and moved back home.

Gary's parents were mortified. They had envisioned a professional future for Gary, maybe medicine or law. Now he was saying that he wanted to become an electrician, an interest he had expressed from an early age but one to which they had given little consideration. Even though they had encouraged Gary to pursue his yen for tinkering in his spare time, they always assumed—or hoped—that his interest in electronics was just a passing phase.

It took two years of bitter fighting and a year of family therapy for Gary to convince his parents that he wanted something different from what they wanted for him. But he finally did—and now, at twenty-six, he is on his way to becoming a certified electrician.

THE SEARCH: WHO, WHEN, AND WHY

The question of whether adoptees should or should not search for their birth parents is one of the most controversial we and other mental health professionals have had to face. On the pro-search side are the arguments that adult adoptees have a right to information about their personal histories, and that it is only by reconnecting with their birth families—either directly or indirectly—that the many questions they grow up with can be satisfactorily resolved.

On the con side are the arguments that birth parents have a right to remain anonymous and to put that part of their past behind them, and that adoptive parents would live under a cloud if they always had to worry that the children they raised would eventually reject them and go back to their birth families.

For some adult adoptees, questions about themselves cannot be answered without finding their birth families. If their search is continually thwarted at every turn, it becomes a looming frustration that stands in the way of their identity formation. Many searchers feel a need to look backward before they can move forward.

> "I hope to find a person that looks like me and who looks at life the way I do," explains Jane, thirty-three. "I want to close the circle of my life."

For others, an activated search would have only a negative effect. Because of the kind of people they are, these people would be threatened by a search; contact with their birth parents would be too disruptive to their sense of themselves as members of their adoptive families.

> "I really am afraid to try to search out my birth mother," says Martin, twenty-seven, "because if I do I might find I don't like her. More importantly, I may find she doesn't like me, and I don't know that I can tolerate another rejection."

Ultimately, we can make only one generalization about searching: it should be up to the adoptee, not up to the whims of adoption agencies or state legislatures or records clerks, whether information about his past becomes available. The relevant question is what the search means to the individual adoptee—and what the adoptee hopes will come out of the search. Why are some adoptees compelled to search for more information about their histories, or for the birth parents themselves? Do they hope to ease their frustrations and disappointments, to undo a sense of rejection? Do they want to reassure their birth mothers that they made the right decision in relinquishing them—or to prove to them that they made the wrong one? Do they want to find new parents, or are they just driven to find someone who looks, feels, laughs, or talks the way they do? How are searchers different from nonsearchers? Are they more troubled, or simply more curious?

Traditional research on searchers helps us make a start at answering these questions.[9] We know from demographic studies that the typical searcher is a young adult—the average age is twenty-nine—and that up to 80 percent of searchers are female. Searchers tend to be married, with stable positions in middle-income jobs. Their interest in searching usually has been triggered by a significant life event: marriage, the birth of a child, the death of one or both adoptive parents.

We are not sure what percentage of adoptees actually mount active searches. As we have indicated, *every* adoptee carries on an intrapsychic search, involving fantasies and curiosity about his birth parents and the reasons for his relinquishment. But relatively few adoptees take that intrapsychic search to the next level, to an activated search either for more specific information or for a reunion with the birth family.

Organizations that keep track of such matters[10] estimate that over the course of a lifetime, 30 to 40 percent of adoptees will eventually search. But we think these figures are too high. These organizations, after all, lobby for open adoption records, so they have a political stake in making searching seem like a popular option. Based on careful studies from Scotland, we estimate that a more realistic figure is closer to 15 percent.[11] As searching becomes more accepted in the adoption community, and as access to previously sealed records becomes easier, this percentage will undoubtedly increase.

The typical searcher is looking for information, not hoping to replace the family that raised and loved him. Fred, for instance, considered his adoption to be highly satisfactory, but he still had this to say about why he wanted to find his birth parents:

"I want to stop running from life, to feel complete, to stop looking at every stranger wondering if I'm related—to settle my self-image anxiety."

The compulsion to search usually says little about the adoptee's satisfaction or dissatisfaction with the adoptive family. Classically, the searcher is looking for a relation, not a relationship; he already has a mother and father. Even after a searcher has found his birth parents, it is still his adoptive parents whom he calls Mom and Dad.

Often a meeting with the birth parents actually brings the adoptee and the adoptive parents closer together. That is what happened to Stuart, who at age twenty-seven mounted a search for his birth mother, with the full cooperation of his parents and his wife. Finding his birth mother, he says, made him love his adoptive parents all the more.

"If I had not been placed for adoption my life would have been rather wretched—an unemployed and essentially homeless mother, who had neither the capacity nor the maturity to have handled an infant," says Stuart. "Through adoption I had a loving, caring, nurturing home that gave me the resources and possibilities to achieve my true potential."

Reunions like Stuart's don't always end happily, however. We know of cases in which a confrontation with a birth mother is terribly traumatic for the adoptee. After years of searching and fantasizing about an affectionate reunion, some adoptees receive nothing from their birth families but an icy stare and an abruptly closed door. Others find their birth mothers to be impoverished or mentally ill. They may be left feeling as damaged themselves as they now perceive their birth mothers to be, or they may suddenly be harassed by birth mothers who see the newly found child as a possible source of financial or emotional support.

We know of other searchers whose relationships with their adoptive parents have been poisoned because of the parents' resentment, anger, and sense of betrayal. Bitter reactions from adoptive parents usually don't stop adoptees from searching; they simply send the search underground, to be carried on without the knowledge of the individuals to whom the adoptee feels closest, his mother and father.

Hank, now thirty-five, discovered he was adopted while going through his mother's papers after her death. Hank was twenty-one. He was stunned, but not particularly angry, but when he asked his father about it he was told, "That's something best left alone. Your mother would have wanted it that way."

At the age of twenty-three, Hank began a search. When his father found out about it he was furious, and extracted Hank's promise not to continue searching, for the sake of his mother's memory. But he did keep searching, in secret, and last year found his biological mother and half brothers, with whom he has made and maintained contact. Hank loves his adoptive father, but he has promised himself never to tell him about this significant event in his life.

Even those searchers who have failed to find a happy ending tend to be satisfied with the process of searching itself. The activated search provides an important psychological function for some people: it allows them to gain control over forces over which they previously had no control. Many adoptees complain about feeling subject to the vicissitudes of a capricious fate—that they were put up for adoption in the first place, adopted by this particular family, denied information about their past. Searching can bring the locus of control from "out there" to "inside" themselves. It allows the adoptee to experience the self as capable of acting rather than being acted upon—a major factor in establishing a healthier identity.

Our own study of ninety-four adult adoptees in search indicates that the process helps them come to grips with at least six universal themes in human development: loss and mourning, envy, sexual identity, consolidation of identity, cognitive dissonance, and body image. These are complicated concepts, and it is worth taking the time to explore them in the context of their meaning for adoptees.

Loss and mourning. The adoptee experiences many losses over a lifetime: the loss of the birth parents, for whom he mourns even if he was placed at birth; the loss of a biological connection to his adoptive parents; the loss of status as a normal member of society with one father and one mother. These feelings often lead to a sense of mourning, of amputation, of vulnerability to potential losses in the future. The adoptee who searches may harbor a variation of the typical family romance fantasy we described in Chapter Three, believing the birth parents to be of humble origin, caring, and exceptionally good.

Eager to confirm their own inherent goodness, and anxious to reassure a birth mother who is imagined to share the adoptee's sense of loss, many searchers express their motivations to search as a way to deal with grief.

> "I wondered if my birth mother was still sad without knowing me and where I was," says Alice, who decided to search in her twenties.

The decision to begin or continue a search is often precipitated by a loss in the adoptee's life, such as the death of an adoptive parent. When adoptive parents die, the adoptee might suddenly feel compelled to put a name and face to the phantom "other" parents who had been companions of his childhood fantasies. He might also suddenly feel free to start searching for his birth parents without hurting his adoptive parents. Since the unconscious knows no time barriers, losses tend to pile up, and the most recent loss drives the adoptee to resolve the first loss, the one that remains potentially reversible. But the literal object of the search, the birth parent, is often the means to another end—an attempt to repair aspects of the self resulting from a feeling of disconnectedness from the human race. As our patient Michael, twenty-eight, has put it,

> "It's a feeling of not being real. I'm like a fictional character in a story, the product of a writer's imagination."

Envy and jealousy. The twin emotions of envy and jealousy often re-emerge for the adoptee during adulthood. As we saw in Chapter Three, psychological development can be seen as the interplay of two forces, envy and jealousy.[12] By envy, we mean the painful awareness of lacking some advantage in comparison with another person, leading to shame, humiliation, fear, outrage, or depression. By jealousy, we mean the feeling that an advantage the person currently has is threatened by a rival. For the adoptee, both envy and jealousy are inevitable, pervasive, and sometimes painful aspects of life with which he must contend throughout the life cycle.

The adoptee continually perceives his differences from the world of the nonadoptee, and at the same time yearns to be the same as others. One way to resolve envy is to eliminate the perceived difference by acquiring the desired advantage. For the adoptee, the advantage is a biological tie; the way to acquire it is through an activated search.

Sexual identity. The complexities of sexual identification for the adopted woman—and the choice between identifying either with an infertile adoptive mother or an unknown birth mother who in fantasy could be promiscuous—often catapult the female adoptee to search. The adopted woman may maintain an inner sense of unreality about the integrity and capacity of her own body, particularly its ability to reproduce. Having no internalized sense of having been born herself, the adopted woman may regard the process of pregnancy and giving birth with foreboding.

"I finally feel able to be a mother myself," said Emily, who successfully searched, "which I couldn't even consider until I found my birth mother."

Sexual development may be compromised, too, in adoptees who fantasize that the reason they were relinquished was that they were of the wrong gender. This fantasy can lead to the adoptee's imitation of the opposite sex, resulting in a confused sexual identity, which again may be resolved after direct contact with the birth mother.

As adoptees reach sexual maturity, the underlying sexual tensions that may occur in the family are different from those that exist in a biological family. Sexual feelings might not be repressed as readily when the incest taboo carries less weight. To deal with these tensions, or the aftereffects of these tensions, some adult adoptees eventually embark on a search for birth parents; they want to know once and for all to whom they are and are not related.

Rarely, rather than resolving problems with sexual identity, the search itself actually leads to new distortions. We have seen three cases in the past three years in which adult children became sexually involved with their birth parents after a successful search. In another case, a twenty-six-year-old male adoptee entered into a year-long affair with his twenty-three-year-old biological sister. In all these cases, the adoptees felt an overwhelming sense of intimacy on finding their relatives—so overwhelming that they felt they had no choice but to act on it sexually. For the first time, they said, they felt truly connected to something, and they were so seduced by the feeling that they crossed some previously sacred moral boundaries. Such a reaction to finding one's birth family is, we must restate, quite rare.

Consolidation of identity. As an adoptee develops an identity—a representation of the self that serves to define him in a variety of social contexts—he often struggles with feelings of duality or duplicity. In this "dual identity" there is a "false" self as an adoptee and a "real" self in relation to the biological family. Through searching, some adoptees seek to reconcile these two sets of perceptions.

> "I need to feel real, to feel that I'm *authentic,*" says our patient Michael, who has been searching for his birth family since he turned eighteen ten years ago. "I want to be like every other human being who knows where he came from and where he belongs. Searching is my way of bringing some substance to who I am."

Consolidation of identity is indeed an all-encompassing theme that runs through every other aspect of the psychological meaning of the search.

Wendy was thirty-seven when she met her birth mother after searching for her for two years. Having been raised in an Orthodox Jewish home, she was intending to emigrate to Israel with her husband and three children, but was surprised to find that her birth mother was not Jewish. This did not trouble her—but it did mean that according to the rabbis in Israel, she could not be considered an Israeli citizen.

> "How could they say I'm not Jewish enough for them!" Wendy said. "I went to religious schools my whole life; I was raised Jewish and I'm raising my own children in the same way."

Her anger at the religious establishment—in which her adoptive parents supported her—served to help Wendy consolidate her identity not only as a woman, a wife, a mother, and a college graduate, but also in some other important ways: as a member of a religious community and as the daughter of her adoptive parents.

Dealing with cognitive dissonance. Cognitive dissonance has been defined as a logical dissimilarity inherent within paired sets of facts a person knows about himself, his behavior, or his environment. Two elements are dissonant if they would not be expected to follow one from the other, and a basic human drive is to relieve this dissonance.

Adoptees in particular have many conflicting elements in their lives. As we saw in our discussion of dialectical thinking, an adoptee's amended birth certificate says he was born to one set of parents, and his own parents tell him he was born to another. He was told he was relinquished because his birth mother loved him, yet he knows from experience that he never wants to be far from the people he loves. He hears from some people that he was a chosen child, yet he hears from others that being adopted is not as good as living with your "real" parents.

The search, then, is an attempt to reconcile cognitive dissonances, to bring order out of a sense of chaos.

"I decided to actually search because I had heard too many stories that clashed together or just didn't make sense," says Joanna. "I wanted to find out the truth—I need to KNOW."

Body image. Beginning in middle childhood and increasing through the vain years of adolescence, physical resemblance (or lack of it) may become a focal point for the adoptee's feelings of isolation. Somewhere out there, he knows, is "a stranger who looks like me," but here instead is an adoptive family with whom any coincidental resemblance is fastened on avidly by casual observers.

"I hated the way people made a big deal of figuring out who I resembled because I desperately wanted to *really* look like someone in my family," says Ginger. "I was constantly searching for someone whom I looked like in any way."

Adoptees cannot take for granted, as biological children can, either similarities or dissimilarities between their bodies and their parents'. As they struggle to imagine what their birth parents look like, they have only their own bodies to go by. But their own body images may be distorted, since they cannot find a biological mirror.

"I had no concept of what I would look like," Susan says, "and I had no one to share concerns unique to my physical self."

Sometimes changes in life events make adoptees focus more than they used to even on issues such as physical appearance. As Jeff's own wedding date approached, for example, he found himself thinking more about ways in which biological family members looked like each other—especially since his own father had remarried and had two biological children with his new wife, after adopting three children with Jeff's mother.

"What struck me is the fact that there is no one in my world who looks like me, other than by coincidence," says Jeff, who is twenty-five and has been told repeatedly that he looks a lot like his father and his younger brother. "There is no one with whom I share blood, genes, traits. It's a little odd, not to have that indisputable bond to one or both of your parents."

Body image may be distorted, too, because it is associated with larger questions of self-esteem. Since the adoptee's infant body was all the birth mother knew of him, the body itself can be associated with relinquishment, and therefore defectiveness.

"All of my life I felt different," says Grace, thirty-three, who has been in and out of therapy for anorexia nervosa and other eating disorders. "Much of my focus has been on my body. I realize now that I was anorexic because I was afraid to grow up. I wanted to be little. I wanted to be loved and cared for by my real mother, and I thought you had to be a child to get that love."

Grace is now of normal weight and has mounted a search for her birth mother.

"The reason I'm searching for her now is not to undo the past," she says, "but to build a future."

People who search are often satisfied with any resolution to the search—a little more information than they had before, a phone call or letter from members of the birth family, an actual meeting with the birth mother, an ongoing relationship, indeed even an outright rejection. They say that the search itself has eased their feelings of differentness and isolation, and any further resolution is just a bonus.

"I don't think I am looking for a mother," says Kelli, twenty-six, who has received detailed information about her biological family and will one day seek out her birth mother in person. "I want information, maybe a friendship. At least I want closure to that part of my life."

In the course of the search, even tiny bits of information take on great weight. When Katherine Maxtone-Graham was thirty-eight, she wrote in *An Adopted Woman*, she discovered that her birth father had been six foot one, with brown hair, blue eyes, and a college degree.

"Just like that you *know* something," Maxtone-Graham wrote. "Not six foot two, not six foot even. Six foot one . . . I could go home, mark a spot on the wall six feet and one inch from the floor and proclaim a victory, 'There, there is my *father.*'"[13]

Kelli, too, was thrilled to receive the information her preliminary searching generated. Inspired by the birth of her son, she realized how important it was for her to learn more about her own heritage.

"The history I got [from the adoption agency] was full of details, even the name I would have had," Kelli says. "I have something of a history, my biological grandfather was straight from Denmark, twins run in my biological family. Having this information meant a lot to me; it made me feel like more of an individual."

That is, after all, the goal for all adoptees getting through this stage of life—to emerge, either with or without an activated search, as a whole, adult individual.

Chapter 6

MID-LIFE

THE FORTIES AND FIFTIES

Beginning in my thirties and forties I really desired to know more about my birth parents, all the where's, when's, and why's. And today I think about it more and more. I see tearful reunions on TV talk shows and in magazines almost every week. It's talked about, not hushed up like it was long ago. They even have birth announcements in the card stores for newly adopted children.

—*Selma, age fifty-seven,*
adopted when she was four weeks old

The forties and fifties are, in many ways, the prime of life. Now is when an individual can reap the fruits of all the hard work of earlier years. Her children are becoming more independent, her career is hitting its stride, her personality has consolidated and matured. During these years, most people reach their peak earning power and achieve—in many aspects of life—their peak performance. Generally, people at this age still have enough youth to be energetic, but already have enough experience to be wise.

In many professions, such as medicine or law or teaching, these years are the most productive and the most rewarding. Airline pilots, according to industry reports, achieve their best safety records in their fifties; when they're older their reflexes are too slow, and when they're younger they lack the experience that will get them out of tough situations.[1]

"Fifty is what forty used to be," said feminist Gloria Steinem on her fiftieth birthday, at a party at the Waldorf-Astoria attended by eight hundred glittering celebrities. "Self-esteem and a measure of success keep us going: not just in our heads but in our bodies."[2]

Whether a body, and a personality, will age well depends on many things. In part, it's simply the luck of the genetic draw; if your parents lived to a ripe old age, you probably will, too. In part, the way someone ages depends on the circumstances of her life. Some of those circumstances are voluntary; decisions made over a lifetime regarding eating, exercising, smoking, and drinking all help determine how long and how well a person will live. And some of those circumstances are involuntary; over the course of a lifetime, good and bad things simply happen to a person and to the people she loves.

Twenty-five years ago, psychologists Thomas H. Holmes and R. H. Rahe of the University of Washington published an article in *The Journal of Psychosomatic Research* that made clear the relationship between life stressors and physical health.[3] A variety of high-stress life events, they found, place individuals at higher-than-normal risk of encountering major health problems. And although negative stressors —such as divorce or the death of a loved one—are most potent in terms of adverse health consequences, even positive experiences like marriage or the birth of a child can be stressful enough to have some adverse impact on health.

Of course, different people cope with stress in different ways, and it's the coping mechanisms that have the biggest impact on physical health. Research on middle-aged adults has shown that those most likely to suffer ill health as a result of life stressors are those with "Type A" behavioral traits: explosive, accelerated speech; impatience with delay; excessive competitiveness; restlessness; undue irritability; and a chronic sense of time urgency. Interestingly, these traits tend to be associated with certain inborn "temperaments" such as the ones we described in Chapter One—leading us to the conclusion that much about the way people react to life events is determined very early on. Psychologists have found that Type A behavior is associated with an early childhood temperament characterized by negative mood, low sensory threshold, low adaptability, and particular activity levels (low activity for males, high for females).[4]

Much about an individual's coping style, temperament, and personality tends to stay stable throughout adulthood. A middle-aged adult usually has the same values and interests that she had in her twenties. This is not to say people are incapable of change, of course; but the changes from early adulthood to middle age occur slowly and the shifts are rarely radical. Even the mid-life crisis, that much-touted reexamination of one's goals and values, is usually resolved by reshaping existing personality traits rather than by completely transforming into a totally "new person."

The way a person copes with stress says a good deal about what her attitude will be about being adopted. Individuals tend to fall into one of two categories in terms of their reaction to life events: they view events as either within their control or not in their control. People who feel internally controlled tend to believe they can take charge and bring about changes in their lives through their own deliberate actions. People who feel externally controlled tend to believe that things happen to them, that they are at the mercy of external events, that their own actions are ineffective at bringing about changes.

In this context, adoption can be seen as a life stressor, and the idiosyncratic ways in which adoptees respond to it can be seen as a reflection of their own coping styles. A good many adoptees consider the stress of adoption to be something they cannot change and would be better off ignoring so they can get on with their lives. These people reveal little inner turmoil about being adopted; they have either suppressed or denied or minimized the significance of adoption in their own lives.

Richard Lazarus, a psychologist at the University of California at Berkeley, has studied the role of coping strategies in handling stress.[5] Denial or avoidance, he says, can be a highly adaptive strategy when the individual is faced with a stressor she cannot change—such as being adopted. In this view, an adoptee who can suppress, avoid, minimize, or deny the significance of being adopted—or even reappraise adoption in a positive light—is able to compartmentalize this aspect of her identity and get on with her life.

We do not want to portray adoptees who suppress or deny any interest in adoption as being maladjusted; denial can be a highly effective coping strategy when confronted with an unchangeable life stressor. But neither do we want to portray these people in denial as being assured of happy lives just because they repress or suppress any interest in adoption or in their origins. This is simply a coping style, and for many people it works—at least until a phone call from a birth mother or the uncovering of a genetic illness makes denial no longer possible.

CONSTRUCTING A LEGACY

One important psychological task during the middle-adulthood years is "generativity," a word Erik Erikson used to describe the urge to leave behind something of yourself—the urge to construct your own legacy. During mid-life, when an individual experiences a growing sense of the foreshortening of time, this legacy building is at its peak.

Generativity can take the form of passing on wisdom to your children, creating works of art or other products that will last, or transmitting ideas to the next generation. Not everyone feels a need to leave behind a piece of herself literally, through sons and daughters. Sometimes being a teacher or an inventor or a mentor or a sculptor can satisfy the same need. A physician we know says he would like to discover a new disease that would be named after him. "My wife has her children and her future," he says, "but I need something tangible—like my name in the medical literature."

Other developmental theorists have outlined psychological tasks facing middle-aged adults that go along with Erikson's crisis of "generativity versus stagnation." Robert Peck, a psychologist at the University of Chicago, describes four major challenges facing individuals in their forties and fifties.[6]

1. Acceptance of the inevitable decline in physical prowess, and greater reliance on mental prowess for life satisfaction.
2. A redefinition of relationships with others, so they become broader, more social, and less sexual.
3. The capacity to shift emotional investment to new people or new activities—an ability Peck calls "cathected flexibility."
4. An ability to remain mentally flexible and open to new experiences or new ways of doing things.

Other thinkers, such as Robert Havighurst of the University of Chicago and Daniel Levinson of Yale, have outlined similar sets of tasks facing the middle-aged adult.[7] Like Peck and Erikson, these other theorists emphasize middle age as a time of continued challenge for the individual. As with any other phase of life, the tasks confronting the mid-life adult might cause her to reexamine her own notions of self, family relations, social interactions, career development, and leisure activities.

The mid-life adult tends to be more tuned in to the needs of others, in large part because of her unique status as negotiator of relationships with two different generations. On the one hand, she is dealing with her aging parents, who are becoming increasingly more dependent while they are letting go emotionally and preparing to face the end of their lives. On the other hand, she is dealing with her adolescent children, who are becoming increasingly more independent while they withdraw emotionally to prepare to face the beginning of their lives as responsible adults. The person caught between these two powerful forces—the aging parent and the emerging child—is in a unique position to give strength and understanding to each.

A person in this so-called sandwich generation can either topple under the weight of these conflicting responsibilities or use her unique position to make sense of her own place in the life cycle. The middle adult years are a period of much self-reflection, a time for thinking about where you have come from, what choices you've made, and whether any of your past choices should be undone.

Unlike the life review of old age, which we will describe in Chapter Seven, the self-reflection of mid-life still allows for some changes. If a person of age forty or fifty feels dissatisfied about the path her life has taken, there is still time to head off in a new direction.

During the middle years, a person undergoes a subtle shift in her notions of time. When she was a child and a young adult, she viewed things from the perspective of the time that had passed since her birth. Now, in middle adulthood, she begins to look at things from the perspective of the time she has left until death. The question used to be, How long have I lived? Now it tends to be, How long do I have left?

This change in time perspective brings on a new urgency to get things done. For people with an unresolved psychological issue—such as is the case with many adoptees, including those who have ignored the issue for most of their lives—this time urgency can tend to crystallize a focus on adoption in a way that had never existed before. Complicating the new interest is the fact that a real clock is ticking; the adoptee's biological parents are aging, too, so this becomes the last chance to find them before it's too late.

An Acceptance About Being Adopted

With this growing sense of urgency about the future, many adoptees turn to the past. The drive toward generativity involves a drive to pass on their own history to the next generation. But if a person is adopted, sometimes her history is a blank wall.

> "Since my adoptive parents have both died, I think every day, 'Who am I?' " says Selma, who is fifty-seven and has searched unsuccessfully for her birth parents for more than fifteen years. "My children have all done family trees in school. I have nothing to tell them that is true . . . I have four grandchildren and the thing that bothers me the most is that I have no medical history for them. I have none to give them except my own."

Individual adoptees react to this gap in their history in idiosyncratic ways. For some, like Selma, it is with a deep sense of loss. But for others—who are not necessarily any "healthier" or more stable, but merely different—this lack of a history can actually be rather exhilarating. Listen, for instance, to Faye, a fifty-eight-year-old homemaker.

> "I am very aware of being only me," says Faye. "I am myself, kind of a really new person."

Faye says she relishes the fact that she has had to invent herself from whole cloth.

The variability of adoptees' coping strategies is difficult to capture in empirical research. Unhappy adoptees are relatively easy to find; satisfied adoptees are not. Content adults do not tend to join adoptees-in-search organizations, which is where most researchers begin when looking for adoptees to study. They do not tend to answer ads, which is where we found many of our own subjects. And they do not tend to be in psychotherapy, another handy spot for seeking out adopted adults to interview.

Since the majority of adoptees are so hard to find, their point of view may be poorly represented in discussions of what it is like to be adopted. We don't know if the members of this vast "silent majority" are truly content about being adopted, or whether they are simply silent.

We have worked hard to seek out individuals who are not searching for their birth parents or experiencing psychological problems that they attribute to being adopted. We have had conversations and correspondence with quite a few such individuals over the years, and their words are instructive.

Claudia, for instance, is a forty-one-year-old university administrator and mother of a twenty-year-old son. She has, as she herself puts it, "a very good sense of self."

"I am a successful administrator, good parent, and have a good marriage," she says. "I can't say that being adopted was positive *or* negative because I never dwelled on the issue. It just *was!*"

Eleanor, a forty-seven-year-old preschool teacher and the mother of two teenagers, is another adult adoptee who seems quite happy with her adoptive status.

"I can summarize my feelings about being adopted in one word— *satisfied*," she says. "I come from a warm and loving family that has always accepted me and made me feel accepted. I couldn't have asked for a better family and I cannot imagine my real family being any better. In fact, given what I know of my biological parents, I certainly feel confident in saying that life would have been much worse had they kept me."

Like every other adult, every adoptee has her own personality, her own way of handling stress, her own way of coping. Much of this is probably determined by genetics, as demonstrated in the compelling work of Thomas Bouchard, a psychologist at the University of Minnesota.[8] Bouchard spent years studying adults who had been separated from their identical twin at birth, most often because each twin was adopted by a different family. The Minnesota group managed to reunite 154 members of 77 twin pairs, almost all of whom had not seen each other since infancy—and some of whom didn't even know they *had* identical twins.

Even though these people had been raised apart, often in very different circumstances, the similarities in about half the subjects were uncanny. Not only did the twin pairs look alike, but they were remarkably alike in intelligence, personality, interests, jobs, marriage choices, even hobbies and habits. One pair of reunited twins, for instance, had both become volunteer firemen and had the habit of flushing the toilet before using it. Another pair both wore four rings on each hand and had married men with the same name.

Bouchard's work was interpreted as supporting the notion that genetic tendencies are more important than environment in determining who it is we become. We strongly adhere to this principle. The inheritability of disorders, traits, interests, and personality is never entirely precise, but we have learned that genetics play a significant role in the development of both certain mental disorders and certain normal personality traits.[9]

Because of the personalities they are born with, some adoptees can take in stride the uncertainties inherent in being adopted. For others, the unknowns of their past loom so large that they become blinded to their own sense of the present or the future.

THE VEIL OF SECRECY

For adoptees now in their forties and fifties, the fact of their adoption was often a deep dark secret that they never found out about until well into adolescence or even adulthood. Many adoptive parents back in the 1930s and 1940s were advised not to tell their children that they were adopted. We have found that it's all too common for adoptees of this generation to have been told about their adoption late in life—and sometimes in some rather traumatic ways.

Even in families that try to keep adoption a secret, the truth almost always comes out eventually. Either some relative makes an idle comment that raises the adoptee's suspicion or the adoptee has always had the uneasy feeling that she wasn't really part of the family. And when the truth does eventually come out, the adoptee's sense of anger and betrayal can be nearly crippling.

"The rage smolders," says Ellen, fifty-eight, whose parents had told her half-truths about her birth history until just two years ago.

"How do I go about forgiving someone who heartlessly denied me getting to know my birth mother, grandfather, aunts, and uncles?"

The effect of this discovery in the middle-adult phase of life can be devastating. Just when individuals are doing the psychological work of synthesizing their histories into some coherent whole to leave behind for future generations, the world comes unglued; nothing is what it had seemed to be. People whose adoption is revealed so late can be left feeling as though their entire upbringing was a sham, as though nothing and no one can be trusted. Childhood events are reanalyzed in light of this new information, and the adult adoptee can be sent into a tailspin.

Laura, a forty-nine-year-old schoolteacher, never suspected she was adopted. But at the age of forty-two, searching out a birth certificate for a passport, Laura found out that she had been adopted in infancy and her extended family had been sworn to secrecy. Her adoptive parents had died years earlier, and it was an aunt who finally admitted the truth.

"I went around looking at mirrors, snapshots, made endless phone calls to surviving relatives, became depressed and very insecure," she remembers. "I consulted a psychologist for two sessions, who let me rant and rave about what had happened to me. She explained that this was trauma and that it would take time to heal my wounds. It took two years until I could discuss my problem without becoming very upset."

Laura says she has never come to terms with being adopted—and has never stopped being angry at the relatives who lied to her.

"I still, after seven years, really feel alone, frustrated, lied to, and like a fish out of water," she says. "My relationships with my aunt and cousins are not what they were in the past. Even though they 'love me,' and are 'family,' my feelings will never be the same."

Sometimes the secretiveness is all-pervasive, as in the case of Mildred. Mildred had felt, throughout her life, that she was adopted; she always thought that important things about her—her looks, her attitudes, her sense of humor—were totally unlike her parents. By the time Mildred was forty-five, her conviction had turned into an obsession. But whenever she asked her mother about it directly, her mother said Mildred absolutely was not adopted. The solution seemed obvious: put Mildred into therapy to try to rid her of this fixation.

Mildred was a patient of a colleague for five years, after which she finally came to accept the fact that her feelings of "being different" from the rest of the family were rooted in her imagination. Three years after her therapy was completed, though, she received a devastating shock. Her mother was dying, and she called Mildred to her deathbed.

"You were right," the old woman said to her daughter, who was by now fifty-eight years old. "You were adopted."

STILL WONDERING AFTER ALL THESE YEARS

Although the most typical time to search for birth parents is the late twenties and early thirties, many adoptees don't feel a need to search until later. The death of their adoptive parents may provide the final impetus to an activated search. The death may make the adoptee feel abandoned and longing for a replacement family; may free the adoptee from feeling guilty about beginning a search; or may enable the adoptee to search without worrying about causing pain to her adoptive parents.

"The death of my adoptive mother," one adopted woman says, "released me from the collusion we both had to deny this elephant in the living room."

Searches may be started in middle life rather than earlier because the individual just didn't have enough time before that. The twenties and thirties are, for many people, occupied with climbing a career ladder and raising a family; neither pursuit leaves much time for personal affairs. But by the fifties, work ambitions may have stilled somewhat, and the children have often left home.

"When raising my four children I was busy, happy, and fulfilled," says Selma, fifty-seven. "I didn't think about being adopted. Now I do."

Selma describes her childhood as "wonderful," but now that her adoptive parents are dead she thinks daily about her birth parents. Her sense of loss is heightened by the death, too, of her best friend, with whom she often talked about being adopted.

"We were close friends all through high school," Selma says, "and after we both married she encouraged me to try and find my birth mother. She and I talked about my adoption a lot. She's passed away now. I miss our talks. I really never confided in anyone else."

The moments for bringing the adoption issue to the surface continue to happen into middle adulthood, sometimes in surprising ways.

"Each time someone we know gives birth and the family begins discussions of who the baby looks like, I have a hunger to know who I look like, even now at this late date," says Donna, age fifty-four. "My older son resembles me, while my younger son looks very much like his father. Who do I look like?"

The issue reemerges for Donna in social conversations, too. She says she could not discuss the "Baby M" surrogate mother case without bursting into tears. In the Baby M case, the woman hired as a surrogate mother refused to relinquish the child to the man who had contracted her services—and whose sperm had been used to artificially inseminate the woman in the first place. As reproductive technology becomes more esoteric, such bizarre quasi-adoptions are likely to make headlines and stir up hidden feelings for many adoptees.[10]

People who decide to search for birth parents often run into obstacles—legal and otherwise—when trying to uncover their own past. For searchers in their forties and fifties, these obstacles are especially frustrating. They may delay the process just long enough for the birth parents to die before they can be found.

"Every day I look in the mirror and I don't know what I am looking at," said Joe Soll, fifty, founder of the Adoption Circle. "Am I
Jewish? Am I Irish? What is my background? I can't conceive of
dying without knowing."

In 1989, after fifteen years of getting nowhere in his search, Joe orga-
nized a national march on Washington to overturn laws sealing adoption records, now on the books in forty-five states.

The question haunting Joe does not go away as he gets older, but
only becomes more basic, stripped to its essentials. He expressed it in
the sign he held aloft at the Washington march. The sign read, "I
wonder who my mommy is."[11]

It took Joe Soll many years to get to the point of adoption activism. He married and divorced twice, never having told his wives that
he was adopted. He entered psychotherapy at the age of thirty-six,
and refused to say the word "adopted" out loud to his therapist—or to
allow her to say the word to him.

"I came close to playing charades to get her to figure out that I was
adopted," he remembers.

Joe was adamant about avoiding the subject altogether.

"I am a crossword puzzle fanatic, and yet when I saw the clue 'Five
letters, to take as one's own,' I threw the puzzle out."

The change in Joe's head-in-the-sand stance came from a chance
remark made by his sister, who was the biological child of his adoptive parents. (She was seven years younger than Joe; a brother, also
his parents' biological child, was five years Joe's junior.) She said casu-
ally that Joe's birth parents might still be alive, since the adoption had
been arranged through a family friend—which stunned Joe, since
their parents had told *him* that his birth parents died in a car crash.

"I asked my mother about the car crash story and she said that it
was a lie that they had been told to tell me," he remembers. Then
he went to his therapist, who badgered him for six months to go
to a meeting of a support group, the Adoptee Liberation Move-

ment Association. When he finally went to an ALMA meeting, "I never felt so accepted anywhere so fast in my life. I actually used the word 'adoption' that very day."

Even for adoptees who never find their birth parents—and probably no more than 10 to 15 percent of adoptees do—our experience has been that people eventually come to their own kind of resolution. Sometimes this resolution is fraught with anger and some bitterness, as in the case of Rita, a fifty-eight-year-old nurse who thinks she has found her birth father.

When she began searching in her forties, Rita found out her birth father was a college student who fell in love with a local maid. After she became pregnant, the father married the birth mother, but they nonetheless decided to relinquish Rita. Then, two years after her birth parents gave her up, Rita found, they had another baby, again a girl— and they gave her Rita's original name.

Rita telephoned the man she believed to be her father. It was not a success.

"He denies any knowledge of anything," she says, "and yet he told me the name I had for my mother was not correct, but similar. It amazes me that he knows that when he knows nothing else." The father asked Rita to stop calling him because she was upsetting his family. "I'm sorry if I upset his family," Rita says, "but he has made my life much more miserable because he won't come forward with any information. I didn't cause this situation, he did."

Rita is resigned to a lifetime of unanswered questions, but she continues to feel, as she puts it, "deprived" of information that could give her some peace.

"I wonder a lot about why I do some of the things I do," she says, "and why I love flowers and my gardening so much. Also I am quite artistic, as is one of my children, and I wonder where that comes from . . . Just knowing some of the facts would give me such peace of mind, something I don't think I will ever experience."

Even without a successful search, the majority of middle-aged adoptees eventually come to terms with uncertainties about their origins. Natalie, for instance, has been searching on and off for her birth parents for nearly thirty-five years. Now fifty-five, she is still filled with unanswered questions, but the urgency of finding answers for them has settled down.

"I'm at peace in a sense," she says, "but I would like to know more. It's not something that is going to drive me wild or anything, but it's an unfinished chapter and I would like to read that last chapter. It's like getting to the end of the book and you have two more pages and you lose the book."

By the age of fifty or so, adoptees who continue to have questions have usually accumulated a lifetime of relationships that minimize the uncertainty of that first relationship with their birth parents. If they have married, had families, have jobs they enjoy, made and kept close friends, then the pain of not knowing their birth families can sometimes be dissipated by the satisfaction of knowing and loving others.

"I will hope till my dying day to know if my birth parents are still alive and where they are, or just to see a picture of them," says Linda, fifty-seven.

But Linda has managed to compartmentalize this mystery and get on with her life.

"My life has been happy and full and I am thankful for that," she says. "I feel very deeply about my family [a husband, two grown children, and one grandchild], and am probably more protective about them and much too sensitive to everything because they are mine."

Chapter 7

LATE ADULTHOOD
THE SIXTIES AND BEYOND

Being adopted has meant for me being a fictitious character in my own life. I have never seriously doubted that I existed; at the same time I have never believed that I was truly the person everybody knew me as. Nobody wanted me as I was; I had to be legally severed from my reality and wrapped in a legal fiction before I could be considered acceptable to society. This does not make for a positive image of oneself.

—Loretta, age sixty-two,
adopted when she was four months old

During old age, the effects of earlier physical and psychological life events culminate in one of two ways: either to provide meaning to a person's life or to induce a sense of despair.

The variability inherent in human development is perhaps most apparent among the aged. The way a person experiences old age depends not only on his innate personality and the events that he has confronted, but—more than during any other period—on the state of his health. People who remain physiologically intact are the most likely to remain psychologically intact.[1]

Difficult as it may be for younger people to believe, old people usually feel as though they are essentially no different than they were forty or fifty or sixty years before.

"I don't feel like an old man," said Bruce Bliven, a writer, when he was eighty-two. "I feel like a young man who has something the matter with him."[2]

In old age, most people try to come to terms with the accomplishments and failures of their lives. This is when pride and disappointment, happiness and grief, discovery and curiosity are somehow blended into a satisfactory whole.

Many of the issues that were important at earlier stages in life are important once again—identity, intimacy, generativity. At the same time, older adults are anticipating their own deaths, not only in a cosmic sense but in a very mundane, pragmatic sense as well. Family ties take on a whole new meaning with the possibility that as people age, the only ones left to take care of them will be members of the family.

Indeed, in some Asian cultures, it is common for older people who have no children of their own to find adults to adopt. These adoptees will be the ones who love and care for them in their old age and pray for them when they are gone.

CHRONOLOGICAL VERSUS PSYCHOLOGICAL AGE

Even more than the middle-aged adult, the older person focuses on the time left to live. Older people tend to date their lives backward, sensing the time remaining rather than calculating the time that has passed. A woman of sixty-five, for instance, usually doesn't think about the fact that sixty-five years have passed since the date of her birth. What she is more aware of is the fact that fifteen years or so are left until the likely date of her death.

This is not necessarily a mournful awareness, though. For many, it is simply a fact of life. As a seventy-eight-year-old woman was quoted as saying in *Ourselves, Growing Older*, a book about aging written by the Boston Women's Health Book Collective,

> "I do not look to the future with dread. It *has* to be shorter than my past, but it does not have to be less rich. I'm more relaxed. I don't try to do everything. That means I can take time for quiet, for meditation, alternate this with activity, and see how I can keep a moving, living balance between the two."[3]

At the same time, the internal sense of how old a person is may often be in conflict with how old he really is, or how old he looks.

Whenever she passes her reflection in a shop window, for example, sixty-six-year-old Clara is stunned.

"I always do a double take," she says. "My first thought is, 'Who is that old woman?' And then, of course, I realize it's me. I may be sixty-six and look sixty-six, but in my mind I'm forever twenty-eight."

Some developmental psychologists, such as John Kotre of the University of Michigan, say the self-image of a person past sixty-five is not as an old person but as an "ageless" person. Agelessness, he says, is part of the self-identity of people like Miriam Cheifetz. Miriam is an eighty-six-year-old widow described in Kotre's book, coauthored with journalist Elizabeth Hall, called *Seasons of Life: Our Dramatic Journey from Birth to Death.*

"I'm a person," insists Miriam. "I'm not an old person, because there are many things about me that are not old—besides my years and the difficulties I have physically. Whatever I am, it has nothing to do with age."[4]

Older people, write Kotre and Hall, strive to preserve this sense of themselves as "ageless" even in the face of undeniable physical decline. "The elderly," they write, "need to marshal whatever energy they have . . . to say, until the last breath of life, 'It's still the same me'—still the same self that was there in the beginning."[5]

The great Russian novelist Leo Tolstoy made the same point about his own old age, a period in which he continued to be artistically productive and politically active.

"I am conscious of myself in exactly the same way now, at eighty-one, as I was conscious of myself, my 'I,' at five or six years of age," Tolstoy wrote in his diary. "Due to this alone there is a movement which we call 'time.' If time moves on, then there must be something that stands still, the consciousness of my 'I' stands still."[6]

Reassuring as consistency is, however, the importance of flexibility and capacity for change is never as great as it is in the final years of life. Without growth and change, there is only stagnation and death.

As gerontologist Robert N. Butler puts it, it is important for the elderly to "loosen up," to go beyond the choices they made earlier in life. "Excessive or exaggerated identity seems clearly to be an obstacle to continued growth and development throughout life and to appreciation of the future," notes Butler, the original director of the National Institute on Aging and now head of the geriatrics department at the Mount Sinai Medical Center in New York. If older people are straitjacketed into the identities or routines established during early or middle adulthood, he says, they may be forced into a rut that has become inappropriate in late adulthood. "I would go so far as to say that a continuing lifelong concern with one's identity is a sign of good health, and the right to have such a concern is one of the important rights of life."[7]

THE TASKS OF OLD AGE: COMING TO TERMS

When he was himself in his eighties, Erik Erikson looked anew at his model of the life cycle. He had been a young man in 1959, when his model was originally published, and his theory of human development reflected his youth. Five of the eight "psychosocial stages of life" took place before the age of twenty.

But in his old age, Erikson began to see the resonances of the last stage of life. In his original model, he characterized old age as the stage in which ego integrity is in conflict with despair. But as an old man, he understood that other conflicts are also important during old age. He wrote in *Vital Involvement in Old Age* (coauthored with his wife, Joan, and psychologist Helen Q. Kivnick) that old age is a time of revisiting every one of the conflicts that had been encountered earlier in the life span.[8] During old age, the prominent conflicts of every other stage—trust versus mistrust, autonomy versus shame and doubt, initiative versus guilt, industry versus inferiority, identity versus confusion, intimacy versus isolation, generativity versus stagnation—occur one final time.

Many developmental psychologists outline specific developmental tasks common in this stage of life. Among them is Robert Peck, a psychologist at the University of Chicago, who says three issues are paramount for the older individual:

- Retirement. A person must redefine himself in areas other than work to face the future with interest, vitality, and a sense of integrity. Hobbies and interests beyond the job help people make a healthy transition to retirement.

- Physical decline. Accommodating to the physical changes of age requires that people shift their values away from the physical domain into the domain of interpersonal relations and mental activities. If their happiness and sense of well-being is derived primarily from the way they look and the way their bodies feel, they are likely to be more disturbed by the physical changes that are inevitable with old age.

- Mortality. Each person in old age must come to grips with his own impending death, not only by accepting the inevitability of fate but by finding meaning in it. This may well be old age's greatest challenge. Peck, like Erikson, believes the answer can be found in the feelings of generativity the individual developed over the years.[9]

Erikson wrote that wisdom, defined as "detached concern with life itself, in the face of death itself,"[10] is the ultimate goal in late adulthood. The attainment of wisdom in old age is a recurrent theme in developmental psychology. In the book *Seasons of Life*, Kotre and Hall describe the work of Marion Perlmutter, a psychologist at the University of Michigan, who defines wisdom as "not just the recognition of repeated patterns in specific domains, but the appreciation of the pattern in life itself." [11] They say Perlmutter has found that wisdom involves "knowing what you don't know, and knowing what is unknowable."

The authors quote Tom Russell, a sixty-four-year-old who sees wisdom as the integration of the emotional and the intellectual.

"There's some things you can't get out of books, you can't get out of computers, you can't get out of anything," Tom says. "They have to come out of the human soul, out of the human mind and heart."[12]

MUSINGS WITH A PURPOSE: THE LIFE REVIEW

A consistent, integrated sense of self over the life span is what Erikson calls "ego integrity," the perspective that your life has been the result of your own actions, that it could not have been a different life, and that it has had meaning. Difficult to achieve, ego integrity is the positive result of a process known as "the life review," the search for pattern and consistency in one's actions over the life span. As people reach the end of their lives, they organize their memories and reinterpret their life experiences.

> "There's a thread that goes through your whole life," notes Miriam Cheifetz in *Seasons of Life*. "And when you see some of that in your own children, you feel that your life was not in vain."[13]

Great artists, not surprisingly, conduct their life reviews artistically. Art historians and musicologists have noted, for instance, that the late-life styles of painters and composers have a certain universal detachment and sense of resolution that seem characteristic of the reflective nature of this stage. Psychologist David L. Gutmann, for instance, made a careful study of the later works of two masters of impressionism, Claude Monet of France and Joseph Mallord William Turner of England. According to Gutmann, both Monet and Turner made "a sharp break from literal representation" as they aged. In their later paintings, "the artist is no longer captured by the immediacy of things but seems to be looking beyond them, trying to picture the primary armatures of reality that lie behind surfaces and appearances."[14]

Similarly, older composers try to get down to universal themes in their music. Dean Keith Simonton, a psychologist at the University of California at Davis, studied the evolving styles of 150 composers and discovered what he called "the swan-song phenomenon." Swan songs, he found, tend to be stripped of flourishes and ornamentation—and probably stripped, too, of whatever fire led to the originality of earlier works—but they are usually the pieces that become the most popular. As described by Kotre and Hall in *Seasons of Life*, swan songs are "expressions of resignation and even contentment in the face of death, [with] no traces of despair. Perhaps, [Simonton] says, as creative artists realize that their careers are coming to a close, they reshape their works-in-progress to produce a final testament."[15]

This may be what most people do, too, in reviewing their own individual works of art: the stories of their lives. That is why the life review is so useful in helping older people achieve a sense of wholeness, of continuity, of satisfaction. Indeed, if the life review does not take place on its own, many psychotherapists guide their older patients through the process to help them come to terms with their personal stories.

As Erikson sees it, the goal of the life review is to see how the story of your life is turning out, to change what can be changed, and to accept the rest. "An essential aspect of what is involved in integrating the final two opposites is a renewed and old-age-specific willingness to remember and review earlier experiences," he writes.[16]

But there may be intermediate—and troubling—steps along the way to acceptance. Some older people, for instance, feel nostalgia tinged with regret as they revisit the choices they made in earlier years. Others go further, feeling anxiety, guilt, depression, despair. Instead of making them feel satisfied and complete, the life review leaves them feeling cheated and enraged.

Adoptees may face a particularly poignant life review, because so many important elements of their earlier lives were beyond their control. Or they may find themselves, in the reflectiveness that often comes with old age, reinterpreting the behavior of the important players in their lives—their birth parents and their adoptive parents. George, for instance, can now reflect on his adoptive mother—who died fifteen years ago—with a new understanding.

> "In these years, as I try to put my life together, I suspect that Mother took adopting a child very seriously," says George, who is sixty-three. "There was a very strong sense in her that she was bringing up somebody else's child and she must do a good job. So that meant I had to perform, or it would bring disgrace on her."

The life review also forces older adoptees to confront one last time the question of how being adopted might have shaped their personalities.

"I believe that I was most affected by a burning desire to excel,"
says Herbert, sixty-six, "in school, in sports, in the Army, in my
business career, and in rearing my family. Perhaps one feels the
initial rejection and then tries harder to please than others . . . I
somehow had a drive that caused me to be successful, perhaps to
say, 'I told you so.' "

SEARCHING: ONE LAST CHANCE

For a variety of reasons, we know even less about older adoptees than
we know about mid-life adoptees. When today's sixty- and seventy-
year-olds were children in the 1920s and 1930s, formal legal adoption
was uncommon. Abandoned babies were either raised by relatives,
cared for in foster homes, or sent to orphanages. And when infants
were adopted, they generally were not told about it—even though
they could have been, since laws that "sealed" adoption records
were not formulated in most states until the late 1940s and early
1950s.

Adopted older adults may feel disconnected from their adoptive
families as well as from their birth families. By this time, no doubt,
both sets of parents have died, as well as many of their birth and
adoptive siblings. So one last time, the adoptee will metaphorically
climb the stairs, open the closet door, and take down the box to deal
with his "issue"—the fact of being adopted. This time, what happens
will be a final understanding of what being adopted has really
meant.

Sometimes it is a specific life event that forces an older adoptee to
confront the issue of adoption. For Shirley, it was her attempt at the
age of sixty-five to register for Social Security benefits—an attempt
that was thwarted because Shirley had no birth certificate.

"I may not get Social Security at all," she says, "and all because of
this stupid secret. Then I get angry, not just about that but about
all the secretiveness over all the years. It's all so totally unneces-
sary, so unkind. When things are kept quiet and whispered about
and never brought out into the open, it always takes on the aura of
something awful."

Loretta's epiphany came when she was sixty years old and hospitalized on the eve of major surgery.

"I *really* realized that I would possibly die without ever having known who I was," Loretta says.

As soon as she recovered from her operation, she went to the adoption agency to seek out more information about her birth family.

And George's self-confrontation came when he realized that searching did not only mean trying to find his birth parents—who in his imagination were never more than "young people who had a baby and gave it away"—but that it could also mean trying to find his birth siblings.

"A friend of mine who was adopted was telling me about how he had made contact with brothers and sisters in his birth family," he says. "All of a sudden I thought, 'My goodness! What if I had a brother or sister?' "

Raised as an only child, George—an ordinarily shy and mild-mannered librarian—was quite startled by the depth of his emotions about searching for siblings.

"I thought that if I knew or had any idea I had brothers or sisters, I couldn't be held down until I found them. It amazed me that I would think that way."

Most older adoptees who search have little hope of actually finding their birth parents, who no doubt have already died.

"Even assuming that my birth mother is still alive," says Loretta, who is now sixty-two, "I don't know how to trace her, or if I want to confront an eighty-five-year-old woman with something she has avoided all her life."

But they may be curious, as George was, about siblings, or they might simply want to find information that would settle some pervasive sense of being unsettled. The search itself, whether or not it leads to a meeting with relatives, allows older people a sense of closure and completion. Unlike the search of young adulthood—when the goal is usually to find blood relatives—a search during old age is a way of bringing to a conclusion the questions that have bothered adoptees their whole lives long.

Shirley, sixty-five, wonders now whether her father's sister—who lived in a distant city, married late, and never had children—could be her birth mother. She imagines a scenario in which the aunt got pregnant and her brother raised the child as his own to help his beloved sister out of her impossible predicament.

"If I did find my aunt was my mother, I would be so much more forgiving," Shirley says. "I would be so much more at peace. There would have been a good reason why she gave me away."

Aside from some physical resemblances to the aunt, Shirley grew suspicious about their real relationship when her aunt, whom Shirley had not seen for many years, called her to her deathbed. Because she does not drive alone and her husband was unwilling to take her, Shirley never made it to her aunt's side.

"But she left me half her estate, in a will that she had written within the year and had witnessed by neighbors. She split everything between a nephew on her husband's side, who lived near her and had taken care of her in her last years, and myself. It seems to me she must have had more than a casual interest in a long-lost niece to have done this. She could have left it all to the nephew."

Searching is especially difficult for adoptees in this generation, since secretiveness about adoption was so pervasive in the 1910s and 1920s. Ida, seventy-six, never even knew she was adopted until she was eighteen, by which time she was married and had a child of her own.

"The kids at school used to ridicule me and poke me and pinch me and call me 'Adopted! Adopted!' " recalls Ida, who began school in about 1920. "The teacher would go home for lunch and I would sit on the seat and cry."

Finally, one lunchtime, Ida grabbed her coat and ran home to ask her mother if what the children said was true.

"She didn't say I was adopted," Ida says, "but she didn't really say I wasn't, neither. She said, 'The Lord gave you to me, I went and got you,' but she didn't say when or where. Then of course she took me up in her arms and sang to me."

It was not until Ida's mother died that her father sat her down and told her that she had in fact been adopted. Interestingly, her reaction was not shock or anger for the secrecy, but merely gratitude at having been raised in a good Christian home. The only scorn she felt was for her birth mother.

"She wasn't a part of me. If she couldn't keep me when I was small, and put me in a shelter with no blanket, I want no part of her."

Although the secretiveness did not trouble Ida, it troubles many of the other adoptees we have met. If adoption has always been treated as an unspeakable secret, the adoptee gets the feeling that being adopted is something horrible and shameful. This feeling begins in childhood and can persist even into old age.

"I remember one day when I was in my teens, and my mother's sister and her children had come for lunch," says Shirley. "My aunt said something to my mother about 'the baby's grave.' I just froze in place; I wanted to run. This was the first I had ever heard about there having been a baby born to my mother who had died."

Much later, Shirley found out that her mother had given birth to a little girl who had died during delivery, her umbilical cord wrapped around her neck. After that, Shirley's parents decided to adopt rather than risk going through such a tragedy a second time.

"It was such a disgrace to me that I was adopted, I didn't want a soul to know," Shirley says. "I didn't want my aunt talking about it in front of my cousins that way, in front of me. Even when I was an adult I felt that way. One time, when my mother was in her seventies, I came to visit her and she was sitting out front with her neighbor. And she was talking about her adopted daughter! I could have died. There I was a married woman, and still I was dropping dead from shame."

Older adoptees may have a rough time going through the life review. As they relive earlier experiences, they are likely to run into a series of unanswered questions: Who were my birth parents? Why did they give me away? What were the first months of my life like? Where did I come from? Even adoptees who have amassed a certain amount of information about their birth histories may have trouble consolidating it all—especially if the information turns out to be different from the fantasies they have lived with their whole lives.

That is what happened to Loretta, who began searching for more information when she was sixty. Loretta had always had an active fantasy life about her birth family, and central to it was the belief that someone in her background was Italian. But when she got her original birth certificate and other information, the truth came out: her mother was an Eastern European Jew, her father a Protestant from Wales.

"Now I felt bereft of my whole fantasized Italian culture," she says. "I didn't know any Welsh people."

Loretta turned to books, poring over literature on Welsh and Celtic culture. What she was looking for, in the seventh decade of her life, was "the foundation for an entirely new fantasy life."

In old age, many individuals begin thinking not only about how they will age but how—and when—they will die. Most biological children have a sort of inner "time bomb" in their heads, an assumption that they will live to roughly the age their parents did. But older adoptees have no such internal clock. As they think about the timing and circumstances of their impending death, they face only uncertainties.

AFTER WINTER, THE SPRING

People who are parents and grandparents have the easiest time of perceiving meaning and continuity to their lives. It is all there: they had children, their children had children, the continuation of their genetic legacy is assured. When older adults also can recognize personality traits and moral values that are passed on to grandchildren, they are especially gratified.

"When I first saw my grandchild I was bursting with joy and pride," a first-time grandmother recalls. "I'd never had a feeling quite like that before . . . to see your own child produce another child and to know that it came through you."[17]

A first-time grandfather had similar emotions:

"I was so happy now that this little grandson would carry on my name, my father's name, this connection between all of us . . . I had been waiting eagerly for a grandchild. I would be a good grandparent to this grandchild, as my grandparents had been to me."[18]

The particular joys of grandparenthood—the ability to nurture a child without taking full responsibility, to love a child unconditionally and then give it back to its parents for the hard work—fulfill an important psychological function for older adults. People are aware of it when they begin to nag their adult children about starting families of their own. "When are you going to have babies?" parents might ask their married children. "I need grandchildren." What they are saying is that they need this sense of their own validation, this confirmation that their genetic material will be carried into the future.

Grandchildren provide this wonderful function for adoptees, too. Natalie, for instance, felt alienated from her adoptive parents, who were strict disciplinarians, and failed in her efforts to find information about her birth parents. Because she feels so alone, her four children and ten grandchildren are especially important to her.

"My life is very, very full," says Natalie, who is fifty-five and a widow. "I had little Michael tonight; I have a commitment to keep him until his dad gets home. So that stroking and that loving that I missed from my adoptive parents, which I didn't find in my marriage either, I get from my grandchildren."

But for adoptees, the gratification of being a grandparent is often tinged with regret. What exactly am I passing along to my grandchildren? they might wonder. What unknown traits from the unknown past might suddenly spring up in the future of these youngsters?

"I truly love my children and grandchildren," says Herbert, who is now sixty-seven and tried for sixteen years to find his birth family. "It caused me great pain when I realized that I couldn't tell them anything about my own family, what nationality I was and when and where I was born. Every American citizen should have the inherent right to know these very intimate facts about his life."

And the intense pleasure of grandparenting can be bittersweet when an older adoptee suddenly finds himself empathizing with his unknown birth parents.

"I have three beautiful grandchildren and am about to have another," says Phyllis, fifty-eight, who says her adoptive parents always made her feel loved and secure. "Once in a while, being a grandmother, I think there may be someone somewhere out there who would be proud of these children."

Because she does not know where she comes from, Phyllis says she thinks of her grandchildren as the sum total of her biological connection to the human race.

Natalie, too, considers it especially important to be biologically tied to her children and grandchildren. Lacking ancestors, she wants to feel connected to her descendants.

"I have a son and three daughters, and I look at them and think, who do they look like? And the same with the grandchildren.

I just search their faces to see what can I see in these little faces."

For all older adults, adopted or not, the later years are a time to come to terms with the life they have lived and to face the certainty of their own mortality. Developmental psychologists have likened the life cycle to the cycle of the seasons, in which the quiet and stagnation of winter gives way to the blossoming growth of spring. The notion of seasons is especially reassuring when considering the close of life, the period that has traditionally been equated with life's winter. The analogy, in the case of human beings, refers to perpetuation of one's own spirit in the descendants who will follow.

Daniel Levinson makes good use of the metaphor of the seasons in his book about the life cycle, which he calls *The Seasons of a Man's Life*. The sequence of seasons is not a hierarchy, writes Levinson, a psychologist at Yale University. A season has no inherent value; it is not necessarily better than the one that came before or worse than the one that will follow. In the same way, he says, a particular age is no better or worse than the age that comes next; it is simply a stage that must be passed through on the way to the end of one cycle and the beginning of another.

"Each season plays its essential part in the unfolding of the life cycle, and the sequence follows a prescribed course," Levinson writes. "Winter is a fallow, quiet time, in which the previous growth comes to an end and the possibility of new growth is created. It is the ultimate transitional period. Unless the creative work of winter is done and the seeds take root, nothing further can grow. Spring is a time of blossoming, when the fruits of winter's labor begin to be realized. The blossoms will not appear unless the seeds have been nourished, and the blossoms in turn make way for the blooming of fully grown flowers."[19]

Part III

CONCLUSIONS

Chapter 8

A LOOK TO THE FUTURE

As our society changes in the twenty-first century, much about adoption is likely to change, too. As family arrangements continue to diverge from the "Mom, Dad, two kids, and dog" nuclear family of the 1950s, being adopted will seem less and less strange. The high divorce rate and prevalence of nontraditional families—stepfamilies, one-parent families, blended families, gay families—will make it more acceptable for an adoptee to have two sets of parents. Many of her classmates, for a variety of reasons, are likely to have two sets of parents also.

The reproductive technologies of the future will also put being adopted into a new context. Side by side with adoptees coming to terms with having been born to unknown parents, we will see people whose parents are every bit as unknown: those conceived through artificial insemination, in vitro fertilization, surrogate mothers, and other conception arrangements we cannot yet foresee. Indeed, as reproductive technology continues to advance, being adopted might come to seem positively tame!

The same social forces that have changed, and will continue to change, the context in which adoption takes place have already altered the nature of adoption itself. As contraception and abortion became commonplace in the 1970s and 1980s, and as illegitimacy and single parenthood more acceptable, fewer healthy newborns have been available for adoption. This means that more of the couples who want to adopt children are turning to nontraditional paths: international adoption, the adoption of older or "special needs" children, privately arranged adoptions, and adoptions in which the birth parents play an active role in raising the child. All of these shifts have changed the way being adopted is experienced in the emerging generation.

The changing face of adoption became clear to us recently when two white gay men came for a consultation. Tony, forty-two, had just adopted a biracial boy who was fifteen months old. His lover, Rick, thirty-five, had contracted with a surrogate mother to bear a child for him, and was now raising the three-year-old twins who had resulted from that birth. Though their family arrangement seemed highly unusual, the two men came to us with a very mundane-sounding question: What should the children call them? Clearly, the "typical" adoptive family isn't what it used to be. (Our advice, by the way, was that the kids call each of them Daddy.)

As the institution of adoption changes, the experience of being adopted will change as well. This limits what we can confidently say about that experience to what we know about *today's* adoptees— though adoption, even as it's currently practiced, is full of variability from one household to the next. As we have noted, the model we have generally used throughout *Being Adopted* is of the "traditional" adoption—one mother, one father, a healthy child of the same race adopted at birth, a birth family about whom very little is known. In this chapter, we intend to make some speculations about the ways in which less "traditional" arrangements will change the experience of being adopted.

These less traditional arrangements fall roughly into three categories: international adoptions, "special needs" adoptions, and open adoptions. Each is likely to have its own effect on the adoptee's experience, so we will consider each in turn.

IMPLICATIONS OF INTERNATIONAL ADOPTIONS

In 1967, the U.S. Immigration and Naturalization Service counted a total of 1,905 children who had been born in foreign countries and adopted by American citizens. By 1987, that figure had increased more than fivefold, with 10,097 foreign-born children adopted in the United States.[1]

The most obvious issue for many of these adoptees is that they cannot escape the fact of being adopted. The great majority of international adoptees are from South Korea, the Philippines, Colombia, Brazil, and India—countries where the prevailing physical characteristics are quite distinct from those of the white Americans who tend to adopt. Many of our young patients who are international adoptees complain that when they walk down the street with their parents, strangers instantly know that they are adopted—they just don't look like part of the family. "It's like living in a fishbowl," a Korean-born teenager has said.

One of our patients, a thirteen-year-old Indian girl from El Salvador, was adopted by a white American couple when she was six years old. As the years went on, the couple came to understand that their daughter had gone through so much pain and trauma in El Salvador that she was suffering from a kind of posttraumatic stress syndrome, with frequent flashbacks of her war-torn childhood. We first met her when she was about ten years old, and she still had a thick Spanish accent. But as her parents were able to work with her and reassure her that she was safe from the nightmares of the past, her accent seemed to disappear, and she began to dress more like a typical American teenager. We have seen this frequently in international adoptees: the more integrated into the family they feel, the more they become a part of the American community.

This is not to say that the goal in international adoption is a family melting pot that denies the adoptee's cultural identity. Indeed, quite the opposite is true. As discussed in Chapter Four, a white family that adopts a nonwhite child from another country must redefine itself as a multiethnic, multiracial family, incorporating the child's culture and holidays into family lore and ritual. To do less would be to deny the adoptee her rightful place in the family.

International adoptions involve not just the loss of culture for the adoptee, but the loss of language, too. We are reminded of a Korean-born patient who was interested in finding his birth mother, but who commented that if he were to meet her, he would need an interpreter. What a poignant statement of how cut off this child feels from his birth family and his origins.

The notion of a search is itself more complicated for international adoptees, since birth records in most of the countries from which children are coming now are virtually nonexistent. Many of these children were left on the doorstep of police stations or on park benches; some were actually kidnapped to be sold to baby brokers. In such cases there are no records to "seal" or "unseal," as there are for American-born adoptees. But even international adoptees can benefit from a search, albeit an indirect one. The adoptee can try to find out more about her birth culture or birth town rather than about who her birth mother is. She can travel to the country where she was born, so she can get an image of what life might have been like for her birth mother. She can visit an orphanage there, too, to answer some questions about what life is like for abandoned children. In these situations, the definition of a successful "search" must be broadened to mean not simply contact with literal blood relatives, but a reconnection with an entire culture.

SPECIAL NEEDS: THE NEW EUPHEMISM

Back in the 1940s and 1950s, social workers used to categorize a certain group of children as "unadoptable." These were the youngsters who were physically or psychologically handicapped, who were black, Hispanic, or biracial, whose parents were in prison or suffering from socially undesirable diseases, who were part of a large sibling group, who were older than about age two—who for one reason or another did not fit the profile of most couples' ideal baby.

In the 1960s, consigning a child to the wastebasket of "unadoptable" was considered politically gauche, so a new euphemism was used: "hard to place." Today these same children—plus legions more who have AIDS, or whose mothers are drug addicts, or who are refugees from international wars—are called "special needs" adoptees.

Special-needs kids often are hooked up with special-needs parents, who for their own part diverge from the traditional agency-approved profile. They include single women, single men, gay couples, biracial couples, people over thirty-five, or couples who already have biological children of their own. The combination of an untraditional child and an untraditional household can at times make adjustment difficult indeed.

This is not to say that special-needs children are always placed in nontraditional families—or that problems necessarily arise when they are. In fact, some anecdotal evidence suggests that these children actually adjust better in unusual family settings, in which parents' expectations are perhaps more flexible.[2]

Special-needs adoptees have often moved from one foster home to another before a permanent family is found for them. This so-called foster care drift can take a terrible toll on children, who may come to doubt their adoptive parents' reassurances that this time it's for good. These children experience loss again and again through multiple separations from foster parents. Their grieving is usually more dramatic and more profound than the grieving of early-placed adoptees. Fortunately, it is also less subtle, and many adoptive parents are able to pick up signs of adjustment problems early and to seek professional help.

In our experience, the hardest time for a "special needs" child to be adopted is between the ages of about six months and three years. Just as the child is forming primary attachments to her caregiver, just as she is developing a sense of trust and security, she is pulled away and placed in a new home. A child of this age is old enough to remember previous attachments, but too young to cope with anger and grief. She lacks the words needed to express her sadness and her fury.

Children older than about age three might have sharper memories of their prior experiences, but they also have more coping skills. In addition, their memories often help them make sense of the reasons for their relinquishment. For some of these late-placed adoptees, who have suffered physical or sexual abuse at the hands of their relatives, the sense of being cut off from their biological families might actually be experienced with relief.

Obviously, a history of sexual abuse in the child complicates the adjustment to being adopted. We think adjustment is further compromised when agencies fail to report the full history to the adoptive parents, either to avoid scaring the parents or to avoid branding the child as destined for trouble. Such failure to provide comprehensive information almost always backfires, however. If the parents are unaware of the child's troubled past, they cannot help the child learn to deal with it and move on.

Even before we discuss whether birth records should be made available to adoptees—and we think they should—we want to emphasize how important it is that these records be thorough, including as much detailed information as possible about the pregnancy and delivery, as well as the child's family life prior to adoption placement. We are coming to recognize the ways in which a high-stress pregnancy—the type that usually precedes a relinquishment—can adversely affect the fetus. Adoptees and their adoptive parents deserve to know to what extent their birth mothers experienced high blood pressure, poor diet, premature labor, and the like. They also deserve to know whether they had low Apgar scores or meconium staining at birth, and whether their first hours of life were marred by problems such as the need for resuscitation or excessive jaundice.

And the sharing of information should not stop at the moment of adoption. No one can anticipate what issues will eventually matter to the adoptee as she ages, so our advice is to provide as many details as possible. One of our patients, for instance, was most interested in finding out where she got her big hands from. Who could have predicted that a question like that would become so meaningful?

We think birth parents should provide ongoing information to be kept in a file for retrieval later—information about what the birth parents are doing now, what they remember about the child, why they decided to relinquish the child, whether they subsequently married and had other children, whether they later developed any genetic diseases, even whether they have big hands or musical talent or the ability to curl their tongues. These small details, if kept somewhere and delivered to the adoptee at the right point in time, could well make the difference between the adoptee feeling rooted and her feeling totally alone.

How Open Is Open Enough?

"Open adoption" is probably the source of greatest controversy among adoption professionals. We see the term as having two components: the opening of records for adult adoptees and for birth parents; and the opening of the relationship between birth parents and adoptive parents from even before the adoptee's birth, with varying degrees of contact and shared information. There is no such thing, at least not this early in its evolution, as a "typical" open adoption. Open adoptions run the gamut from those that involve a minimal sharing of nonidentifying information to those in which the birth mother is taken care of during her pregnancy right under the adoptive family's roof.

On the question of opening birth records to adult adoptees, we feel very little ambivalence: it simply should be done. These records, after all, are about the adoptee, and we are troubled by the idea that some hospital clerk or agency social worker stands between those records and the person for whom they can do the most good.

Adoption records are sealed by law in about forty-five states. The most common argument for the sealing of records has been to preserve the confidentiality of the birth mother. We think this argument is spurious, for several reasons. In the first place, not every birth mother wants anonymity—even those who might have wanted it when they first gave up their babies. Many successful searchers we know discovered that even though their birth mothers requested anonymity at the time of birth, they subsequently changed their minds and were relieved to have been found. Over time these birth mothers had developed a longing to find out how their baby was doing; as each birthday passed, the curiosity grew. But there is currently no easy way for a birth mother to indicate that she no longer wants her identity concealed from her child. Hospital records clerks simply see the "sealed" marked across the birth records, and have no way of knowing how the mother feels now.

When proponents of sealed records talk about preserving the birth mother's confidentiality, we are struck by how little confidentiality even exists in the first place. Many people know exactly who the birth mother is: adoption agencies, baby brokers, the courts—everyone, it seems, but the adoptee. Many people have full access to these records, but the individual to whom the records rightfully belong does not.

We are also struck by how little concern is voiced, in this vigorous debate about sealed records, for the point of view of the adoptee herself. We have a tradition in our judicial system of holding paramount "the best interest of the child." And yet the sealing of adoption records—which in our view is clearly contrary to the child's best interest—is being defended in terms of the best interest of the two sets of parents. We hope to see a return to the adoptee as the central figure in these discussions.

The relative weight that should be given to the adoptee's interest, in comparison to those of the adoptive parents and the birth parents, is much like the relative length of the hypotenuse in comparison to the length of the two other sides of a right triangle. Remember the Pythagorean theorem from elementary geometry? We think it works nicely in the "adoption triangle," too.

The Pythagorean theorem states that

$$A^2 + B^2 = C^2$$

in which A and B are the two shortest sides of a right triangle and C is the longest side, the hypotenuse. In our theorem, we have used a new mnemonic device:

$$A = \text{Adoptive Parents}, \quad B = \text{Birth Parents}, \quad C = \text{Child}$$

This is, we believe, a nice way to illustrate just how much the needs of the child outweigh those of either set of parents.

This simple fact is easy to ignore, especially since the policymakers tend to represent only one portion of the equation. We know many legislators at the local, state, and national levels who are adoptive parents, but we know very few who are adoptees, and not a single one who admits to being a birth parent.

Another reason why we think birth records should be unsealed has more to do with a moral imperative than a mental health one. All citizens have a right to know about themselves. Any nonadoptee can simply write to the bureau of vital statistics in the state in which she was born and receive her birth certificate. We think adoptees should be able to get their own birth records just as easily.

And while we're on the subject of release of information, we want to make a case for better training for all professionals involved in adoption. Training programs in psychiatry, child psychiatry, psychology, and social work include little information about how early life experiences might affect an adopted child's development. Even those who work day in and day out with adoptees may be sadly lacking in the training they need. One of our patients, an eleven-year-old girl who was adopted at birth, was said by the agency that placed her to have had an absolutely normal delivery. But she developed problems during her childhood, and her parents, both well-educated professionals, eventually sought psychiatric help. Only then did the information come out that there had been meconium (stool from the fetus) in the amniotic fluid at the time of birth. This is a classic indication of stress during delivery, and is often a red flag for learning or emotional problems during childhood. But the agency caseworker did not know that. She had not passed on the information to the parents, she said, because she didn't think it was important.

To sum up our feelings about unsealing birth records, then: for those people who want it, it's crucial to give all parties involved the chance to find out more about their hidden past. Ignorance about the past provides an extraordinarily fertile field for fantasies, many of them the kind that interfere with psychological growth. Not knowing does not allow things to settle inside; it merely stirs things up. Our experience has been that people who are troubled about adoption almost always feel better after making connections with their birth families, even if in doing so they have uncovered some disturbing truths.

This brings us to the second part of the "openness" trend: adoptions that are "open" from the very beginning. Open adoptions range from limited contact between adoptee and birth parent, usually through an intermediary, all the way to the extreme of direct contact at the time of birth or even before. In some open adoptions, such as the one described by Lincoln Caplan in his book *An Open Adoption*, the birth parents select the couple they want to raise their baby, the birth mother lives with the adoptive parents during her pregnancy (in the case of Caplan's subjects, she lived with the adoptive parents' best friends), and the adoptive parents act as birth attendants during labor and delivery.[3] After relinquishment—an informal ceremony in which the birth mother physically hands the baby to the adoptive parents—the birth mother may take on the status of a favored aunt. She may send letters, photos, and gifts; she may visit; she may even baby-sit.

We reserve judgment on what this unprecedented openness will mean for the adoptee. The practice is too new, and the children are too young—the oldest of them are just entering adolescence—for us to know precisely how such contact with the birth mother will change the experience of being adopted. While we know that problems have been associated with traditional adoption, no one has been able to document that open adoption is free of those problems, or that it doesn't create some problems of its own. So at the risk of generating a good deal of controversy in this already controversial area, we would like to offer a few cautious speculations.

On the positive side, we think, open adoption can eliminate the secretiveness and fear of the unknown that have proved so debilitating for some adoptees. If you know your birth mother, you don't have to spend your time walking down the street and wondering if you'll run into her. When you have questions about why she gave you up, or whether she was artistic like you, or whether cancer runs in the family, you can simply ask her. And since the relationship between the child and the adoptive parents is based upon openness and honesty, that relationship may benefit, too.

On the con side, frequent contact with the birth mother may increase a child's confusion and anxiety. If she gave you away, what is she doing here? If she is here, can she take you back? During times of conflict, the young child might feel torn between two sets of parents. Later, as she becomes more skilled at manipulating her parents, the child may play off one set of parents against the other, just as she would if she were caught between two families after a divorce. It is not uncommon for the adoptive parents in open adoptions to terminate the relationship with the birth mother when things get too complicated, which could generate a new set of feelings of loss and betrayal.

Until researchers are able to follow the children of open adoption in sizable numbers over a long period of time, we will not know just how the practice affects adoptees. The first books on the subject, such as *Children of Open Adoption* by Kathleen Silber and Patricia Martinez Dorner, are limited to the first wave of children, most of whom are still under ten.[4] These children are not only very young, but they are probably being raised in highly unusual families. As happens in any innovation, the pioneers of open adoptions are a very select group of parents: highly educated, liberal, open-minded, nondefensive, experimental individuals who are not tied to traditional mores and lifestyles. These adoptive parents, and the birth parents involved in open adoption, tend to be willing to deal with moral ambiguity and complexity. If open adoption proves a good solution for them, however, it does not necessarily follow that it would be good for everyone.

The need for an individualistic approach to adoption, both now and in the future, is one we want to emphasize one last time. People are unique in terms of their inborn temperaments, life experiences, and coping styles, and the particular combination that arises in a particular individual will help determine what being adopted means to her. To impose a single system onto human beings, who are so idiosyncratic, cannot possibly work for everyone. We do not recommend a system that is entirely open any more than we approve of the system that is entirely closed. Members of the adoption triangle deserve a flexible, responsive system that allows them to choose how much information they want—and the freedom to change their minds at any point along the way.

In the future, as the very practice of adoption becomes more and more variable, these individual differences among different adoptive families will be even greater than it is today. We can only hope that the system devises the mechanisms that will be needed to accommodate those differences.

EPILOGUE:
ONE LIFE REVIEW

As an example of how being adopted affected one individual over a life span, we present the brief autobiography of Bertha. She is a seventy-three-year-old retired schoolteacher who was adopted in infancy.

I was adopted seventy-three years ago. Such a long time ago. I can't remember when I first knew I was adopted. There doesn't seem to be a specific time when my mother or father told me. It's like I always knew, like it was just a part of me from the beginning.

I do have memories, though, of times when my mother would talk to me about it. One time was when I was about five. I remember because we brought home a puppy that day from a neighbor's farm. My mom told me that the puppy was ours now and I would be its mother—an adoptive mother just like she was. I remember feeling good about that because we were the same—adoptive mothers.

My memories of being adopted when I was small are mostly positive. There were times when others teased me ("You're adopted, you're adopted, you're adopted"), and, of course, it kind of hurt, but these times were few in number.

I didn't have many people to talk to about being adopted. I was an only child. Sometimes my mother and I would talk. Not much, but occasionally. She seemed to be comfortable about it. So was I. Dad didn't talk much about it. But then, he wasn't much of a talker.

When I was about nine years old, I remember reading a book about a little girl who lived with people who were not her parents. The girl was very sad about being separated from her mother and father and tried to run away to find them. I remember asking my mother about my first mother and father—those who made me and gave me life. I remember thinking about what they might be like. I think it was the first time I ever consciously did that—think about what they were like. I wasn't terribly sad. Just sort of confused. I remember thinking that they might miss me. That made me uncomfortable.

When I was a teenager, one of the girls at school got pregnant. It was a scandal. She was sent away to an aunt in another state. I was told that she put the baby up for adoption. She never came back to live in our area. I remember how it hit me—that's what happened to my first mother and to me. I remember getting mad when I heard that she gave the baby away. But then I realized that she couldn't help it. It was best for the baby and for her.

Probably the most difficult time for me regarding adoption was when I got married and had my own children. When my first child was born I looked at her and realized there was no way in the world that I could ever be apart from her. I think this was the worst time for me. It brought up a lot of feelings about having been "given away." Intellectually, I knew there was little choice for my mother—the stigma and all about illegitimacy during those times. But emotionally, it was difficult to take. Could there be a legitimate reason for me to give up my baby? Never!!! Then how could there be a legitimate reason for Mother to give me up? I don't know whether it was post-partum depression or the adoption issue, but for a few months after my baby was born, I was really out of sorts—depressed, angry, irritable. It passed, though, as all things do.

When I got older and my children were grown, they sometimes asked about my adoption. They seemed to be more interested than I was about my background—of course, it was their biological background, too. My daughter urged me to search for my relatives. Sometimes I wanted to, but I just never got around to doing it. I had a little information about them—the town they were from and some specifics about what they did. It was a small town and I'm sure that it wouldn't have been too difficult to find out more, if not actually find them. I think I was scared—about what I would find out. Would I be welcomed? Did I want to be? It was very confusing to me.

My husband urged me to leave well enough alone. My daughter pushed me to search. I felt trapped in the middle. When my mother died, my adoptive mother, I almost went through with it. I realized that one thing that had been holding me back all these years was my concern about the effect it would have on my parents. Yet even though I felt freer to search after my mother died, I still didn't do it—I'm not really sure why.

As I look back over my life, I realize that being adopted has had some effect on me. But it has been quite small compared to everything else. There have been sad times, confusing times, times of curiosity, and angry times. Most of all, adoption has just been a fact of life—a kind of backdrop in my life. Always there, but simply taken for granted.

NOTES

Prologue

1. Viorst, Judith, *Necessary Losses*. New York: Simon and Schuster, 1986.
2. Community residents who responded to our newspaper advertisements were asked to write autobiographical sketches detailing their thoughts, feelings, and experiences about being adopted. To help them with this task, we provided them with a series of questions that could be used as a starting point. Some individuals chose to respond quite directly to these questions, with little elaboration, whereas others went well beyond the scope of our questions. All individuals were informed beforehand that the information provided would be used in the development of this book, as well as for research purposes. They also were told that all identifying information would be deleted or altered to insure confidentiality.

Introduction

1. Bohman, Michael, "A Comparative Study of Adopted Children, Foster Children and Children in Their Biological Environment Born After Undesired Pregnancies," *Acta Paediatrica Scandinavica* (Suppl. 221), 1–38, 1971.
2. David, Henry P., *Born Unwanted: Developmental Effects of Denied Abortion*. New York: Springer Publishers, 1988.
3. Kadushin, A., *Child Welfare Services* (3d ed.). New York: Macmillan, 1980.
4. Brodzinsky, David M., "Adjustment to Adoption: A Psychosocial Perspective," *Clinical Psychology Review*, vol. 7, pp. 25–47, 1987.
5. Ibid.
6. Among the most important of these studies are Bohman, *Adopted Children and Their Families: A Follow-Up Study of Adopted Children, Their Background Environment, and Adjustment*, Stockholm: Proprius, 1970; Brodzinsky, Radice, Huffman, and Merkler, "Prevalence of Clinically Significant Symptomatology in a Nonclinical Sample of Adopted and Nonadopted Children," *Journal of Clinical Child Psychology*, vol. 16, pp. 350–56, 1987; Brodzinsky, Schechter, Braff, and Singer, "Psychological and Academic Adjustment in Adopted Children," *Journal of Consulting and Clinical Psychology*, vol. 52, pp. 582–90, 1984; Dalby, Fox, and Haslam, "Adoption and Foster Care Rates in Pediatric Disorders," *Developmental and Behavioral Pediatrics*, vol. 3, pp. 61–64, 1982; Deutsch, Swanson, Bruell, Cantwell, Weinberg, and Baren, "Over-representation of Adoptees in Children with Attention Deficit Disorder," *Behavior Genetics*, vol. 12, pp. 231–38, 1982; Fullerton, Goodrich, and Berman, "Adoption Predicts Psychiatric Treatment Resistances in Hos-

pitalized Adolescents," *Journal of the American Academy of Child Psychiatry*, vol. 25, pp. 542–51, 1986; Hoopes, *Prediction in Child Development: A Longitudinal Study of Adoptive and Nonadoptive Families*, New York: Child Welfare League of America, 1982; Schechter, Carlson, Simmons, and Work, "Emotional Problems in the Adoptee," *Archives of General Psychiatry*, vol. 10, pp. 37–46, 1964; and Ternay, Wilborn, and Day, "Perceived Child-Parent Relationships and Child Adjustment in Families with Both Adopted and Natural Children," *Journal of Genetic Psychology*, vol. 146, pp. 261–72, 1985.

7. Kirschner, David, "The Adopted Child Syndrome: A Study of Some Characteristics of Disturbed Adopted Children," *Report of the South Shore Institute for Advanced Studies*, Merrick, N.Y., 1980. Also David Kirschner and Linda Nagel, "Antisocial Behavior in Adoptees: Patterns and Dynamics," *Child and Adolescent Social Work*, vol. 5, no. 4, pp. 300–14, 1988.

8. Brodzinsky, David M., et al., "Prevalence of Adoptees in Special Education Populations," *Journal of Learning Disabilities*, in press. Also Brodzinsky, Radice, Huffman, and Merkler, "Prevalence of Clinically Significant Symptomatology in a Nonclinical Sample of Adopted and Nonadopted Children," *Journal of Clinical Child Psychology*, vol. 16, pp. 350–56, 1987.

9. Zill, Nicholas, "Behavior and Learning Problems Among Adopted Children: Findings from a U.S. National Survey of Child Health." Paper presented at the meeting of the Society for Research in Child Development, Toronto, April 1985.

10. Bohman, Michael, and Sören Sigvardsson, "Outcome in Adoption: Lessons from Longitudinal Studies," in Brodzinsky and Schechter, eds., *The Psychology of Adoption*, New York: Oxford University Press, 1990, pp.93–106.

11. Hoopes, Janet, op. cit. Also Sorosky, Baran, and Pannor, "Identity Conflicts in Adoptees," *American Journal of Orthopsychiatry*, vol. 45, pp. 18–27, 1975; and "Adoption and the Adolescent: An Overview," in Feinstein and Giovacchini, eds., *Adolescent Psychiatry*, vol. 5, New York: Jason Aronson, 1977.

12. Sants, H. J., "Genealogical Bewilderment in Children with Substitute Parents," *British Journal of Medical Psychology*, vol. 37, pp. 133–41, 1964.

13. Erikson, Erik H., *Identity and the Life Cycle: Selected Papers by Erik H. Erikson: Vol. 1, Psychological Issues*, New York: International Universities Press, 1959; and *Childhood and Society*, New York: W. W. Norton, 1950.

14. Brodzinsky, David M., "Adjustment to Adoption."

15. Silber, Kathleen, and Patricia Martinez Dorner, *Children of Open Adoption*. San Antonio, Tex.: Corona Publishing Company, 1990.

CHAPTER ONE: INFANCY

1. Kirk, H. David, *Shared Fate*, Glencoe, Ill.: The Free Press, 1964; and *Adoptive Kinship: A Modern Institution Is in Need of Reform*, Toronto: Butterworth, 1981.

2. Erikson, Erik H., *Childhood and Society*. New York: W. W. Norton, 1950.

3. Stern, Daniel, *The Interpersonal World of the Infant: A View from Psychoanalysis and Developmental Psychology*. New York: Basic Books, 1985, pp. 26–28.

4. Katz, Sanford N., introduction to John Triseliotis, *In Search of Origins: The Experiences of Adopted People*. Boston: Beacon Press, 1973, p. xi.

5. Singer, Brodzinsky, Ramsay, Steir, and Waters, "Mother-Infant Attachment in Adoptive Families," *Child Development*, vol. 56, pp. 1543–51, 1985.

6. Klaus, Marshall, John Kennel, et al., "Maternal Attachment—Importance of the First Postpartum Days," *The New England Journal of Medicine*, vol. 286, pp. 460–63, 1972.

7. Lorenz, Konrad Z., "Der Kumpan in der Umwelt des Vogels," *Journal of Ornithology, Leipzig*, vol. 83, 1935. English translation in C. Schiller, ed., *Instinctive Behaviour*. New York: International University Presses, 1957.

8. MacFarlane, J., "Olfaction in the Development of Sound Preferences in the Human Neonate," in M. Hofer, ed., *Parent-Infant Interaction*. Amsterdam: Elsevier, 1975.

9. Bowlby, John, *Attachment and Loss. Vol. 1: Attachment*. New York: Basic Books, 1969.

10. Bowlby, John, *The Making and Breaking of Affectional Bonds*. London: Tavistock Publications, 1979, p. 111.

11. Ainsworth, Blehar, Waters, and Wall, *Patterns of Attachment: A Psychological Study of the Strange Situation*. Hillsdale, N.J.: Erlbaum, 1978.

12. Ainsworth, Mary D. S., "Infant-Mother Attachment," *American Psychologist*, vol. 34, pp. 932–37, 1979.

13. Lewis, Feining, McGuffay, and Jaskin, "Predicting Psychopathology in Six-year-olds from Early Social Relations," *Child Development*, vol. 55, pp. 123–36, 1984.

14. Singer, Brodzinsky, Ramsay, Steir, and Waters, "Mother-Infant Attachment in Adoptive Families," *Child Development*, vol. 56, pp. 1543–51, 1985.

15. Yarrow and Goodwin, "The Immediate Impact of Separation: Reactions of Infants to a Change in Mother Figure"; and Yarrow, Goodwin, Manheimer, and Milowe, "Infancy Experiences and Cognitive and Personality Development at 10 Years," both in Stone, Smith, and Murphy, eds., *The Competent Infant*. New York: Basic Books, 1973.

16. Justin Call's work is described in Melina, Lois Ruskai, *Raising Adopted Children: A Manual for Adoptive Parents*. New York: Harper and Row, 1986, p. 17.

17. Thomas, Alexander, and Stella Chess, *Temperament and Development*. New York: Brunner/ Mazel, 1977.

18. Kirk, H. David, op. cit., 1964.

19. Brodzinsky, D. M., "Adjustment to Adoption: A Psychosocial Perspective," *Clinical Psychology Review*, vol. 7, pp. 25–47, 1987.

20. Katz, Sanford N., op. cit., p. xi.

21. Hoopes, Janet L., *Prediction in Child Development: A Longitudinal Study of Adoptive and Nonadoptive Families*. New York: Child Welfare League of America, 1982.

22. Schechter, Carlson, Simmons, and Work, "Emotional Problems in the Adoptee," *Archives of General Psychiatry*, vol. 10, pp. 37–46, 1964.

23. Kirk, H. David, op. cit., pp. 162–63.

Chapter Two: Toddlerhood and Preschool

1. Bertenthal, B., and Fischer, K., "Development of Self-recognition in the Infant," *Developmental Psychology*, vol. 14, pp. 44–50, 1978; Lewis, M., and Brooks-Gunn, J., *Social Cognition and the Acquisition of the Self*, New York: Plenum, 1979.

2. Stern, Daniel N., *The Interpersonal World of the Infant*. New York: Basic Books, 1985, p. 28.

3. Kagan, Jerome, *The Second Year: The Emergence of Self-awareness*. Cambridge: Harvard University Press, 1981.

4. Mahler, Pine, and Bergman, *The Psychological Birth of the Human Infant*. New York: Basic Books, 1975.

5. Erikson, Erik H., *Childhood and Society* (2d ed.). New York: W. W. Norton, 1963.

6. Piaget, Jean, *The Child's Conception of the World*. New York: Harcourt Brace, 1929.

7. Milne, A. A. *Winnie-the-Pooh*. New York: E. P. Dutton, 1926, pp. 5–6.

8. Brodzinsky, Singer, and Braff, "Children's Understanding of Adoption," *Child Development*, vol. 55, pp. 869–78, 1984; Brodzinsky, Schechter, and Brodzinsky, "Children's Knowledge of Adoption: Developmental Changes and Implications for Adjustment," in Ashmore and Brodzinsky, eds., *Thinking About the Family: Views of Parents and Children*, Hillsdale, N.J.: Erlbaum, 1986.

9. Singer, Brodzinsky, Ramsay, Steir, and Waters, "Mother-Infant Attachment in Adoptive Families," *Child Development*, vol. 56, pp. 1543–51, 1985.

10. Huffman, Loreen, "The Relationship Between Maternal Belief Systems Concerning Adoption with Child Adjustment at Four Years of Age." Unpublished master's thesis, Rutgers University, 1988.

CHAPTER THREE: MIDDLE CHILDHOOD

1. Tanner, J. M. *Fetus into Man: Physical Growth from Conception to Maturity*. Cambridge: Harvard University Press, 1978.

2. Broughtman, John, "Development of Concepts of Self, Mind, Reality, and Knowledge," in W. Damon, ed., *Social Cognition: New Directions for Child Development*. San Francisco: Jossey-Bass, 1978.

3. Coopersmith, Stanley, *The Antecedents of Self-esteem*. San Francisco: Freeman, 1967.

4. Singer, Brodzinsky, and Braff, "Children's Belief About Adoption: A Developmental Study," *Journal of Applied Developmental Psychology*, vol. 3, pp. 285–94, 1982.

5. We asked our research subjects whether adoptees were more likely, less likely, or equally likely to exhibit various traits as compared to nonadoptees. A total thirty-two questions were designed, covering such areas as intellectual and academic competence ("Who is more likely to learn things easily?"), social relationships ("Who is more likely to make friends easily?"), emotional adjustment ("Who is more likely to be sad?"), morality ("Who is more likely to cheat at games?"), and self-concept and self-esteem ("Who is more likely to feel sure of himself?").

6. Piaget, Jean, and Barbel Inhelder, *The Child's Construction of Quantities: Conservation and Atomism*. New York: Basic Books, 1974.

7. Brodzinsky, Singer, and Braff, "Children's Understanding of Adoption," *Child Development*, vol. 55, pp. 869–78, 1984; Brodzinsky, Schechter, and Brodzinsky, "Children's Knowledge of Adoption: Developmental Changes and Implications for Adjustment," in Ashmore and Brodzinsky, eds., *Thinking About the Family: Views of Parents and Children*, Hillsdale, N.J.: Erlbaum, 1986.

8. In addition, a background of neglect such as Curtis experienced, as well as a background of abuse, often sets the stage for experiencing more abuse in the future. Dr. Bernard Berliner, a psychiatrist in private practice in San Francisco, has described how such an upbringing leads to a tendency toward what is called a sado-masochistic relationship.

9. Fenichel, O., *The Psychoanalytic Theory of Neurosis*. New York: W. W. Norton, 1945, p. 96.

10. Freud, Sigmund, "Family Romances," in J. Strachey, ed. and trans., *The Standard Edition of the Complete Psychological Works of Sigmund Freud*, vol. 9. London: Hogarth Press, 1959 (originally published in 1914).

11. Wieder, Herbert, "The Family Romance Fantasies of Adopted Children," *Psychoanalytic Quarterly*, vol. 46, 1977, pp. 185–200. Wieder tells of Jeannie, adopted at birth, who at the age of nine began to tell stories about three little chicks who almost starved to death because their mother was not there to feed them. The chicks were in danger of being sold and eaten, but they were rescued by a nice lady. "Sometimes I think of who made me," Jeannie said, "and I hate being given away. My [adoptive] mommy wouldn't give me away. She saved me." Wieder has two other papers relating to this issue: "On Being Told of Adoption," *Psychoanalytic Quarterly*, vol. 46, pp. 1–22, 1977, and "On When and Whether to Disclose About Adoption," *Journal of the American Psychoanalytic Association*, vol. 26, pp. 793–811, 1978.

12. Kirk, H. David, *Shared Fate*, Glencoe, Ill.: Free Press, 1964; and *Adoptive Kinship: A Modern Institution Is in Need of Reform*, Toronto: Butterworth, 1981. Kirk's theories have been criticized by Kaye and Warren, "Discourse About Adoption in Adoptive Families," *Journal of Family Psychology*, vol. 1, pp. 406–33, 1988.

13. Gormly, Anne V., and David M. Brodzinsky, *Lifespan Human Development*, 4th ed. New York: Holt Rinehart and Winston, 1989, p. 254. Adapted from the *Diagnosis and Statistical Manual* 3-R. Washington, D.C.: American Psychiatric Association, 1987.

14. Technically, attention deficit hyperactivity disorder (ADHD) is *not* a learning disability. However, as researchers and clinicians have observed, it is commonly associated with learning disabilities. Furthermore, it is found more often in adopted children, especially boys, than nonadopted children (cf., Deutsch, Swanson, Bruell, Cantwell, Weinberg, and Baren, "Overrepresentation of Adoptees in Children with the Attention Deficit Disorder," *Behavior Genetics*, vol. 12, pp. 231–38, 1982).

15. Deutsch, Swanson, Bruell, Cantwell, Weinberg, and Baren, "Overrepresentation of Adoptees in Children with the Attention Deficit Disorder," *Behavior Genetics*, vol. 12, pp. 231–38, 1982; Horn and Turner, "Minnesota Multiphasic Personality Inventory Profiles Among Subgroups of Unwed Mothers," *Journal of Consulting and Clinical Psychology*, vol. 44, pp. 25–33, 1976.

CHAPTER FOUR: ADOLESCENCE

1. LeShan, Eda, *How to Survive Parenthood*. New York: Random House, 1965.

2. Offer, Daniel, *The Psychological World of the Teenager: A Study of Normal Adolescence*. New York: Basic Books, 1969.

3. Pumpian-Mindlin, Eugene, "Omnipotentiality, Youth, and Commitment," *Journal of the American Academy of Child Psychiatry*, vol. 4, pp. 1–18, 1965.

4. Marcia, James E., "Development and Validation of Ego-Identity Status," *Journal of Personality and Social Psychology*, vol. 3, pp. 551–58, 1966; "Ego Identity Status: Relationship to Change in Self-esteem, 'General Maladjustment,' and Authoritarianism," *Journal of Personality*, vol. 38, pp. 119–33; "Identity in Adolescence," in J. Adelson, ed., *Handbook of Adolescent Psychology*, New York: Wiley, 1980.

5. Not to minimize the close relationship between mind and body, we hasten to point out that Joe's unusual growth pattern might also have been determined genetically. Had he and his parents known the men in Joe's biological family tended to grow very slowly and then shoot up in late adolescence, they all might have been more comfortable about his apparent growth retardation. This is another case in which more open access to information about birth parents would have allayed many concerns.

6. Once again, we need to emphasize that some of these responses depend on the inborn

temperament of the child. Issues that might deeply trouble one adolescent might present no problem at all for another adolescent—even one raised in the same home—who was born with a less sensitive constitution.

7. As the debate about nature versus nurture rages on, we find that Sharon's story about the uncanny resemblance between adoptees and their birth parents is not at all unusual. We have attended many meetings of adoption support groups in which the adoptees display pictures of their biological relatives and point with great pride to similarities. It is our firm and repeated observation that there are amazing similarities thus displayed, not just physically—including not only appearance but tendencies to certain illnesses, wake-sleep patterns, or allergies—but in terms of personality as well. Over and over again we hear adoptees talk about sharing with their birth parents the same sense of humor, favorite foods, hobbies, and habits.

8. Krementz, Jill, *How It Feels to Be Adopted*. New York: Alfred A. Knopf, 1982, p. 61.

CHAPTER FIVE: YOUNG ADULTHOOD

1. Gould, Roger, *Transformations: Growth and Change in Adult Life*. New York: Simon and Schuster, 1978.

2. Kiley, Dan, *The Peter Pan Syndrome: Men Who Have Never Grown Up*. New York: Dodd, Mead and Company, 1983.

3. Keniston, Kenneth, "Youth: A 'New' Stage of Life," *The American Scholar*, pp. 631–50, Autumn 1970; and *Youth and Dissent: The Rise of a New Generation*, New York: Harcourt Brace Jovanovich, 1971.

4. Havighurst, Robert J., "Youth in Exploration and Man Emergent," in H. Burrow, ed., *Man in a World of Work*, Boston: Houghton Mifflin, 1964; and *Developmental Tasks and Education* (3d ed.), New York: McKay, 1974 (Table 5).

5. Riegel, Klaus F., "Dialectic Operations: The Final Period of Cognitive Development," *Human Development*, vol. 16, pp. 346–70; and Kramer, D. A., "Post-formal Operations? A Need for Further Conceptualization," *Human Development*, vol. 26, pp. 91–105, 1983.

6. Rosenberg, Maxine B., *Growing Up Adopted*. New York: Bradbury Press, 1989, p. 29.

7. Gilligan, Carol, *In a Different Voice: Psychological Theory and Women's Development*. Cambridge: Harvard University Press, 1982.

8. Scarr, S., and K. Kidd, "Developmental Behavior Genetics," in Haith and Campos, eds., *Handbook of Child Psychology: Vol. 2, Infancy and Developmental Psychobiology*, New York: Wiley, 1983; Cadoret, Remi J., "Biologic Perspectives of Adoptee Adjustment" in Brodzinsky and Schechter, eds., *The Psychology of Adoption*, New York: Oxford University Press, 1990, pp. 25–41; Plomin, DeFries, and Loehlin, "Genotype-Environment Interaction and Correlation in the Analysis of Human Behavior," *Psychological Bulletin*, vol. 84, pp. 309–27, 1977.

9. Schechter, Marshall D., and Doris Bertocci, "The Meaning of the Search," in Brodzinsky and Schechter, eds., *The Psychology of Adoption*. New York: Oxford University Press, 1990.

10. Among the organizations that keep track of such figures are the Adoptee Liberation Movement Association (ALMA), Adoption Forum, Adoptees in Search, Adoption Circle, Orphan Voyage, Yesterday's Children, and American Adoption Congress.

11. Triseliotis, J., *In Search of Origins: The Experience of Adopted People*. London: Routledge and Kegan Paul, 1973.

12. Anderson, Robert E., "Envy and Jealousy," *Journal of College Student Psychotherapy*, vol. 1, pp. 49–81, 1987.
13. Maxtone-Graham, Katherine, *An Adopted Woman*. New York: Remi Books, p. 10, 1983.

CHAPTER SIX: MID-LIFE

1. Pesmen, Curtis, *How a Man Ages*. New York: Ballantine Books/Esquire Press, 1984.
2. Henig, Robin Marantz, *How a Woman Ages*. New York: Ballantine Books/Esquire Press, 1985.
3. Holmes and Rahe, "The Social Readjustment Rating Scale," *Journal of Psychosomatic Research*, vol. 11, pp. 213–18, 1967.
4. Rosenman, Ray, and M. Friedman, "Relationship of Type A Behavior Pattern to Coronary Heart Disease," in Hans Selye, ed., *Selye's Guide to Stress Research*, Vol. 2. New York: Scientific and Academic Editions, 1983.
5. Lazarus, R. S., and S. Folkman, *Stress, Appraisal and Coping*. New York: Springer, 1984.
6. Peck, Robert, "Psychological Development in the Second Half of Life," in B. L. Neugarten, ed., *Middle Age and Aging*. Chicago: University of Chicago Press, 1968.
7. Havighurst, Robert J., *Developmental Tasks and Education* (3d ed.), New York: McKay, 1974; Levinson, Daniel, *The Seasons of a Man's Life*, New York: Alfred A. Knopf, 1979.
8. One of the best summaries of Thomas Bouchard's work appears in *Discover*, September 1987; "The Eerie World of Twins" by Clare Mead Rosen.
9. Years ago a psychiatrist at Downstate Medical Center in Brooklyn had the chance to see many adopted twins in his preschool who were being raised by different parents. What amazed him, well before Bouchard's work, was that while the twins generally acted quite like their adoptive parents, in times of stress the twin pairs behaved more like each other than like either adoptive family.
10. The Baby M case, for which we were asked to write expert opinions, ended with the Supreme Court of New Jersey granting primary custody of the child, a girl, to the father and his wife, with limited contact granted to the surrogate mother. The case evoked enormous reactions from both adoptive parent groups and birth parent groups around the world. It clearly challenged adoptive parents' rights, and highlighted the dilemma of birth mothers, who often felt powerless over a system that seemed more concerned with desires of adoptive parents than those of birth parents.
11. Dzik, Eileen, "Digging for their Roots," *The Washington Post*, p. B5, August 8, 1989.

CHAPTER SEVEN: LATE ADULTHOOD

1. Eisdorfer, Carl, and Frances Wilkie, "Stress, Disease, Aging, and Behavior," in Birren and Schaie, eds., *Handbook of the Psychology of Aging*. New York: Van Nostrand Reinhold, 1977.
2. Kotre, John, and Elizabeth Hall, *Seasons of Life: Our Dramatic Journey from Birth to Death*. New York: Little, Brown, 1990, p. 370.
3. Boston Women's Health Book Collective, *Ourselves, Growing Older*. New York: Simon and Schuster, 1987, p. 390.
4. Kotre and Hall, op. cit., p. 372.
5. Ibid.
6. Cited in Butler, Robert N., *Why Survive? Being Old in America*. New York: Harper and Row, 1975, p. 401.

7. Ibid.
8. Erikson, Erik, Joan Erikson, and Helen Q. Kivnick, *Vital Involvement in Old Age.* New York: W. W. Norton, 1986.
9. Peck, Robert, "Psychological Development in the Second Half of Life," in Neugarten, B., ed., *Middle Age and Aging.* Chicago: University of Chicago Press, 1968.
10. Erikson, Erikson, and Kivnick, op. cit., p. 39.
11. Kotre and Hall, op. cit., pp. 375–76.
12. Ibid., p. 375.
13. Ibid., p. 369.
14. Gutmann, David L., "Psychoanalysis and Aging: A Developmental View," in Greenspan and Pollock, eds., *The Course of Life.* Washington, D.C.: National Institute of Mental Health, 1980, pp. 489–517.
15. Kotre and Hall, op. cit., p. 378.
16. Erikson, Erikson, and Kivnick, op. cit., p. 40.
17. Kornhaber, Arthur, and Kenneth L. Woodward, *Grandparents/Grandchildren.* New York: Doubleday, 1981, p. 53.
18. Ibid., p. 54.
19. yyLevinson, Daniel, *The Seasons of a Man's Life.* New York: Alfred A. Knopf, 1979, p. 319.

CHAPTER EIGHT: A LOOK TO THE FUTURE

1. Register, Sherri, *Are Those Kids Yours?* New York: Free Press, 1991, p. 3.
2. As illustrated by H. David Kirk in his book *Shared Fate* (Glencoe, Ill.: Free Press, 1964), the child and family in any adoption are brought together by their mutual needs. In the case of "hard to place" adoptees who are matched with nontraditional parents, the needs involved are highly idiosyncratic, which often makes for a more intense bond.
3. Caplan, Lincoln, *An Open Adoption.* New York: Farrar, Straus and Giroux, 1990.
4. Silber, Kathleen, and Patricia Martinez Dorner, *Children of Open Adoption.* San Antonio, Tex.: Corona Publishing, 1990.

BIBLIOGRAPHY

Allen, Elizabeth Cooper, *Mother, Can You Hear Me?* New York: Dodd, Mead, 1983.

Barth, Richard, and Marianne Berry, *Adoption and Disruption: Rates, Risks, and Responses.* New York: Aldine de Gruyter, 1988.

Benet, M. K., *The Politics of Adoption.* New York: Free Press, 1976.

Bohman, Michael, *Adopted Children and Their Families: A Follow-Up Study of Adopted Children, Their Background Environment, and Adjustment.* Stockholm: Proprius, 1970.

Boswell, J., *The Kindness of Strangers.* New York: Pantheon Books, 1988.

Brodzinsky, David M., and Marshall D. Schechter, eds., *The Psychology of Adoption.* New York: Oxford University Press, 1990.

Caplan, Lincoln, *An Open Adoption.* New York: Farrar, Straus and Giroux, 1990.

Festinger, Trudy, *Necessary Risk: A Study of Adoptions and Disrupted Adoptive Placements.* Washington, D.C.: Child Welfare League of America, 1986.

Figelman, W., and A. R. Silverman, *Chosen Children.* New York: Praeger, 1983.

Hartman, Ann, *Working with Adoptive Families Beyond Placement.* New York: Child Welfare League of America, 1984.

Hoffman-Riem, Christa, *The Adopted Child: Family Life with Double Parenthood.* New Brunswick, N.J.: Transaction Press, 1990.

Hoopes, Janet, *Prediction in Child Development: A Longitudinal Study of Adoptive and Nonadoptive Families.* New York: Child Welfare League of America, 1982.

Jewett, Claudia, *Adopting the Older Child.* Harvard, MA: Harvard Common Press, 1978.

Kadusin, Alfred, *Adopting Older Children.* New York: Columbia University Press, 1970.

Kirk, H. David, *Adoptive Kinship: A Modern Institution Is in Need of Reform.* Toronto: Butterworth, 1981.

————, *Shared Fate.* Glencoe, Ill.: The Free Press, 1964.

Komar, Miriam, *Communicating with the Adopted Child.* New York: Walker and Company, 1991.

Krementz, Jill, *How It Feels to Be Adopted.* New York: Alfred A. Knopf, 1982.

Ladner, Joyce, *Mixed Families: Adopting Across Racial Boundaries.* New York: Anchor Press/Doubleday, 1977.

Lifton, Betty Jean, *Lost and Found: The Adoption Experience.* New York: Dial Press, 1979.

————, *Twice Born: Memoirs of an Adopted Daughter.* New York: McGraw-Hill, 1975.

Lindsay, J. W., *Open Adoption: A Caring Option.* Buena Park, Calif.: Morning Glory Press, 1987.

McRoy, Ruth, Harold Grotevant, and Louis Zurcher, *Emotional Disturbance in Adopted Adolescents: Origins and Development.* New York: Praeger, 1988.

McRoy, Ruth, and Louis Zurcher, *Transracial Adoptees: The Adolescent Years.* Springfield, Ill.: Charles C. Thomas, 1983.

McWhinnie, *Adopted Children and How They Grow Up.* London: Routledge and Kegan Paul, 1967.

Marcus, C., *Who Is My Mother?* Toronto: Macmillan, 1981.

Maxtone-Graham, Katherine, *An Adopted Woman.* New York: Remi Books, 1983.

Melina, Lois Ruskai, *Raising Adopted Children: A Manual for Adoptive Parents.* New York: Harper and Row, 1986.

Nelson, Katherine, *On Adoption's Frontier: A Study of Special Needs Adoptive Families.* New York: Child Welfare League of America, 1985.

Nickman, Steven, *The Adoption Experience.* New York: Julian Messner, 1985.

Paton, Jean M., *The Adopted Break Silence.* Philadelphia: Life History Study Center, 1954.

————, *Orphan Voyage.* New York: Vintage, 1968.

————, *Three Trips Home.* Action, Calif.: Life History Center, 1960.

Powell, John, *Whose Child Am I? Adults' Recollections of Being Adopted.* New York: Teresias Press, 1985.

Prentice, C. S., *An Adopted Child Looks at Adoption.* New York: Appleton-Century, 1940.

Raynor, L., *The Adopted Child Comes of Age*. London: George Allen and Unwin, 1980.

Riben, M., *Shedding Light on the Dark Side of Adoption*. Detroit: Harlow, 1988.

Rillera, Mary Jo, and Sharon Kaplan, *Cooperative Adoption*. Westminster, Calif.: Triadoption Publications, 1984.

Rosenberg, Maxine B., *Growing Up Adopted*. New York: Bradbury Press, 1989.

Sachdev, P., ed., *Adoption: Current Issues and Trends*. Toronto: Butterworth, 1984.

Schaffer, Judith, and Christina Lindstrom, *How to Raise an Adopted Child*. New York: Crown Publishers, 1989.

Siegel, Stephanie, *Parenting Your Adopted Child*. New York: Prentice Hall Press, 1989.

Silber, Kathleen, and Patricia Martinez Dorner, *Children of Open Adoption*. San Antonio, Tex.: Corona Publishing, 1990.

Silber, Kathleen, and Phylis Speedlin, *Dear Birthmother*. San Antonio, Tex.: Corona Publishing, 1983.

Simon, R., and H. Alstein, *Transracial Adoptees and Their Families*. New York: Praeger, 1987.

Sorosky, Arthur D., Annette Baran, and Reuben Pannor, *The Adoption Triangle*. New York: Anchor Press/Doubleday, 1978.

Stein, L., and J. Hoopes, *Identity Formation in the Adopted Adolescent*. New York: Child Welfare League of America, 1985.

Tizard, Barbara, *Adoption: A Second Chance*. New York: Free Press, 1978.

Triseliotis, John, *In Search of Origins: The Experience of Adopted People*. Boston: Beacon Press, 1973.

————, ed., *New Developments in Foster Care and Adoption*. London: Routledge and Kegan Paul, 1980.

Winkler, R., D. Brown, M. Van Keppel, and A. Blanchard, *Clinical Practice in Adoption*. New York: Pergamon Press, 1988.

INDEX

ABOUT THE AUTHORS

DAVID M. BRODZINSKY, PH.D., is Associate Professor of Clinical and Developmental Psychology at Rutgers University. He has an active private practice in which he specializes in treating adoptees, adoptive parents, and birth parents, and is also a forensic psychologist who often testifies in adoption and child custody cases, including the noted "Baby M" surrogate-mother trial. With Marshall Schechter, he is coeditor of *The Psychology of Adoption* (Oxford University Press, 1990), and he is also the author of numerous professional publications on adoption and other areas of child development.

MARSHALL D. SCHECHTER, M.D., is Professor Emeritus of Child and Adolescent Psychiatry at the University of Pennsylvania. He previously held professorships at the University of California at Los Angeles, the University of Oklahoma, and the State University of New York Medical School in Syracuse. For the past forty-plus years, he has had a psychiatric practice in which he has concentrated on adoption issues, including direct patient care of adoptees, birth parents, and adoptive parents, adoption research, agency consultations, and developing pre- and postadoption services. He has also made major contributions in the areas of learning disabilities, attention deficit hyperactivity disorder, and normal development and forensic issues.

ROBIN MARANTZ HENIG, a nationally known medical writer, is the author of three previous books: *The Myth of Senility* (Anchor Press/Doubleday, 1981; Scott Foresman/AARP Books, 1985, 1988), *Your Premature Baby* (Rawson Associates, 1983; Ballantine Books, 1984), and *How a Woman Ages* (Ballantine Books, 1985). She is a frequent contributor to general-interest magazines, including *The New York Times Magazine*, *Vogue*, and *Mirabella*, and is currently working on a book about new virus diseases.